All Things are Possible

ALL THINGS ARE POSSIBLE

ALL THINGS ARE POSSIBLE
BY LEO SHESTOV

AUTHORISED TRANSLATION
BY S. S. KOTELIANSKY
WITH A FOREWORD BY
D. H. LAWRENCE

LONDON: MARTIN SECKER

First published in England, 1920

NOTE

LEO SHESTOV is one of the living Russians. He is about fifty years old. He was born at Kiev, and studied at the university there. His first book appeared in 1898, since which year he has gradually gained an assured position as one of the best critics and essayists in Russia. A list of his works is as follows :—

1898. Shakespeare and his Critic, Brandes.

1900. Good in the Teaching of Dostoevsky and Nietzsche : Philosophy and Preaching.

1903. Dostoevsky and Nietzsche : The Philosophy of Tragedy.

1905. The Apotheosis of Groundlessness (here translated under the title " All Things are Possible ").

1908. Beginnings and Ends.

1912. Great Vigils.

FOREWORD

*In his paragraph on The Russian Spirit,
Shestov gives us the real clue to Russian
literature. European culture is a rootless
thing in the Russians. With us, it is our
very blood and bones, the very nerve and root
of our psyche. We think in a certain fashion,
we feel in a certain fashion, because our whole
substance is of this fashion. Our speech and
feeling are organically inevitable to us.*

*With the Russians it is different. They
have only been inoculated with the virus of
European culture and ethic. The virus works
in them like a disease. And the inflammation
and irritation comes forth as literature. The
bubbling and fizzing is almost chemical, not
organic. It is an organism seething as it
accepts and masters the strange virus. What*

7

the Russian is struggling with, crying out against, is not life itself: it is only European culture which has been introduced into his psyche, and which hurts him. The tragedy is not so much a real soul tragedy, as a surgical one. Russian art, Russian literature after all does not stand on the same footing as European or Greek or Egyptian art. It is not spontaneous utterance. It is not the flowering of a race. It is a surgical outcry, horrifying, or marvellous, lacerating at first; but when we get used to it, not really so profound, not really ultimate, a little extraneous.

What is valuable, is the evidence against European culture, implied in the novelists, here at last expressed. Since Peter the Great Russia has been accepting Europe, and seething Europe down in a curious process of katabolism. Russia has been expressing nothing inherently Russian. Russia's modern Christianity even was not Russian. Her genuine Christianity, Byzantine and Asiatic, is incomprehensible to us. So with her true philosophy. What she has actually uttered

8

is her own unwilling, fantastic reproduction of European truths. What she has really to utter the coming centuries will hear. For Russia will certainly inherit the future. What we already call the greatness of Russia is only her pre-natal struggling.

It seems as if she had at last absorbed and overcome the virus of old Europe. Soon her new, healthy body will begin to act in its own reality, imitative no more, protesting no more, crying no more, but full and sound and lusty in itself. Real Russia is born. She will laugh at us before long. Meanwhile she goes through the last stages of reaction against us, kicking away from the old womb of Europe.

In Shestov one of the last kicks is given. True, he seems to be only reactionary and destructive. But he can find a little amusement at last in tweaking the European nose, so he is fairly free. European idealism is anathema. But more than this, it is a little comical. We feel the new independence in his new, half-amused indifference.

He is only tweaking the nose of European

9

idealism. He is preaching nothing: so he protests time and again. He absolutely refutes any imputation of a central idea. He is so afraid lest it should turn out to be another hateful hedge-stake of an ideal.

" Everything is possible "—this is his really central cry. It is not nihilism. It is only a shaking free of the human psyche from old bonds. The positive central idea is that the human psyche, or soul, really believes in itself, and in nothing else.

Dress this up in a little comely language, and we have a real new ideal, that will last us for a new, long epoch. The human soul itself is the source and well-head of creative activity. In the unconscious human soul the creative prompting issues first into the universe. Open the consciousness to this prompting, away with all your old sluice-gates, locks, dams, channels. No ideal on earth is anything more than an obstruction, in the end, to the creative issue of the spontaneous soul. Away with all ideals. Let each individual act spontaneously from the forever-incalculable

10

prompting of the creative well-head within him. There is no universal law. Each being is, at his purest, a law unto himself, single, unique, a Godhead, a fountain from the unknown.

This is the ideal which Shestov refuses positively to state, because he is afraid it may prove in the end a trap to catch his own free spirit. So it may. But it is none the less a real, living ideal for the moment, the very salvation. When it becomes ancient, and like the old lion who lay in his cave and whined, devours all its servants, then it can be despatched. Meanwhile it is a really liberating word.

Shestov's style is puzzling at first. Having found the " ands " and " buts " and " becauses " and " therefores " hampered him, he clips them all off deliberately and even spitefully, so that his thought is like a man with no buttons on his clothes, ludicrously hitching along all undone. One must be amused, not irritated. Where the armholes were a bit tight, Shestov cuts a slit. It is baffling, but

1·1

really rather piquant. The real conjunction, the real unification lies in the reader's own amusement, not in the author's unbroken logic.

D. H. Lawrence.

PART I

Zu fragmentarish ist Welt und Leben.

H. HEINE.

THE obscure streets of life do not offer
the conveniences of the central thorough-
fares : no electric light, no gas, not even a
kerosene lamp-bracket. There are no pave-
ments : the traveller has to fumble his
way in the dark. If he needs a light, he
must wait for a thunderbolt, or else,
primitive-wise, knock a spark out of a
stone. In a glimpse will appear unfamiliar
outlines ; and then, what he has taken in
he must try to remember, no matter whether
the impression was right or false. For he
will not easily get another light, except he
run his head against a wall, and see sparks
that way. What can a wretched pedestrian
gather under such circumstances ? How
can we expect a clear account from him
whose curiosity (let us suppose his curiosity so strong) led him to grope his way
among the outskirts of life ? Why should
we try. to compare his records with those of
the travellers through brilliant streets ?

The law of sequence in natural phenomena seems so plausible, so obvious, that
one is tempted to look for its origin, not
in the realities of actual life, but in the
promptings of the human mind. This law
of sequence is the most mysterious of all
the natural laws. Why so much order ?
Why not chaos and disorderliness ? Really,
if the hypothesis of sequence had not
offered such blatant advantages to the
human intelligence, man would never have
thought of raising it to the rank of eternal
and irrefutable truth. But he saw his
opportunity. Thanks to the grand hypothesis, man is forewarned and forearmed.
Thanks to this master-key, the future is at
his mercy. He knows, in order that he
may foreknow : *savoir pour prévoir*. Here,
is man, by virtue of one supreme assumption, dictator henceforward of all nature.
The philosophers have ever bowed the knee
to success. So down they went before the
newly-invented law of natural sequence,
they hailed it with the title of eternal truth.
But even this seemed insufficient. *L'appétit
vient en mangeant.* Like the old woman in
the fairy-tale about the golden fish, they
had it in their minds that the fish should

do their errands. But some few people at last could not stand this impudence. Some very few began to object. . . . .

3

The comfortable settled man says to himself: "How could one live without being sure of the morrow; how could one sleep without a roof over one's head?" But misfortune turns him out of house and home. He must perforce sleep under a hedge. He cannot rest, he is full of terrors. There may be wild beasts, fellow-tramps. But in the long run he gets used to it. He will trust himself to chance, live like a tramp, and sleep his sleep in a ditch.

4

A writer, particularly a young and inexperienced writer, feels himself under an obligation to give his reader the fullest answers to all possible questions. Conscience will not let him shut his eyes to tormenting problems, and so he begins to speak of "first and ultimate things." As he cannot say anything profitable on such subjects—for it is not the business of the young to be profoundly philosophical— he grows excited, he shouts himself to hoarseness. In the end he is silent from exhaustion. And then, if his words have had any success with the public, he is astonished to find that he has become a prophet. Whereupon, if he be an average sort of person, he is filled with an insatiable desire to preserve his influence till the end of his days. But if he be more sensitive or gifted than usual, he begins to despise the crowd for its vulgar credulity, and himself for having posed in the stupid and disgraceful character of a clown of lofty ideas.

5

How painful it is to read Plato's account of the last conversations of Socrates! The days, even the hours of the old man are numbered, and yet he talks, talks, talks. . . . Crito comes to him in the early morning and tells him that the sacred ships will shortly return to Athens. And at once Socrates is ready to talk, to argue. . . . It is possible, of course, that Plato is not altogether to be trusted. It is said that Socrates observed, of the dialogues already written down by Plato. "How much that youth has belied me!" But then from all sources we have it, that Socrates spent the month following his verdict in incessant conversations with his pupils and friends. That is what it is to be a beloved master, and to have disciples. You can't even die quietly. . . . The best death is really the one which is considered the worst : to die alone, in a foreign land, in a poor-house, or, as they say, like a dog under a hedge. Then at least one may spend one's last moments honestly, without dissembling or ostentation, preparing oneself for the dreadful, or wonderful, event. Pascal, as his sister tells us, also talked a great deal before his death, and de Musset cried like a baby. Perhaps Socrates and Pascal talked so much, for fear they should start crying. It is a false shame !

6

The fact that some ideas, or some series of ideas, are materially unprofitable to mankind cannot serve as a justification for their rejection. Once an idea is there, the gates must be opened to it. For if you close the gates, the thought will force a way in, or, like the fly in the fable, will sneak through unawares. Ideas have no regard for our laws of honour or morality. Take for example realism in literature. At its appearance it aroused universal indigna-

19

tion. Why need we know the dirt of life ?
And honestly, there *is* no need. Realism
could give no straightforward justification
for itself. But, as it had to come through,
it was ready with a lie; it compared itself
to pathology, called itself useful, beneficial,
and so obtained a place. We can all see
now that realism is *not* beneficial, but-harm-
ful, very harmful, and that it has nothing
in common with pathology. Nevertheless,
it is no longer easy to drive it from its
place. The prohibition evaded, there is
now the *justus titulus possessionis*.

7

Count Tolstoy preached inaction. It seems
he had no need. We " inact " remarkably.
Idleness, just that idleness Tolstoy dreamed
of, a free, conscious idling that despises
labour, this is one of the chief characteristics
of our time. Of course I speak of the higher,
cultured classes, the aristocracy of spirit—
" We write books, paint pictures, compose
symphonies "—But is that labour ? It is
only the amusement of idleness. So that
Tolstoy is much more to the point when,
forgetting his preaching of inaction, he
bids us trudge eight hours a day at the tail
of the plough. In this there is some

sense. Idleness spoils us. We were re-
turning to the most primitive of all the
states of our forefathers. Like paradisal
Adam and Eve, having no need to sweat
for our bread, we were trying to pilfer the
fruit from the forbidden tree. Truly we
received a similar punishment. Divine laws
are inscrutable. In Paradise everything is
permitted, except curiosity. Even labour
is allowed, though it is not obligatory, as it
is outside. Tolstoy realised the dangers of
the paradisal state. He stooped to talk of
inaction for a moment—and then he began
to work. Since in regular, smooth, constant, rhythmical labour, whether it is
efficient or whether it merely appears efficient,
like Tolstoy's farming, there is peace of
mind. Look at the industrious 'Germans,
who begin and who end their day with a
prayer. In Paradise, where there is no
labour, and no need for long rest and heavy
sleep, all temptations become dangerous.
It is a peril to live there. . . . Perhaps
present-day people eschew the paradisal
state. They prefer work, for where there
is no work there is no smoothness, no
regularity, no peacefulness, no satisfaction.
In Eden, even the well-informed individuals
cannot tell what will come next, *savoir*

pour prévoir does not answer, and everlasting laws are exposed to ridicule. Amongst ourselves also a few of the work-abjurors, the idlers, are beginning to question our established knowledge. But the majority of men, and particularly Germans, still defend *a priori* judgments, on the ground that without these, perfect knowledge would be impossible, there could be no regulation of the course of natural phenomena, and no looking ahead.

8

To escape from the grasp of contemporary ruling ideas, one should study history. The lives of other men in other lands in other ages teach us to realise that our " eternal laws " and infallible ideas are just abortions. Take a step further, imagine mankind living elsewhere than on this earth, and all our terrestial eternalities lose their charm.

9

We know nothing of the ultimate realities of our existence, nor shall we ever know anything. Let that be agreed. But it does not follow that therefore we must accept some or other dogmatic theory as a *modus vivendi*, no, not even positivism, which has such a sceptical face on it. It only follows that man is free to change his conception of the universe as often as he changes his boots or his gloves, and that constancy of principle belongs only to one's relationships with other people, in order that they may know where and to what extent they may depend on us. Therefore, on principle man should respect order in the external world and complete chaos in the inner. And for those who find it difficult to bear such a duality, some internal order might also be provided. Only, they should not pride themselves on it, but always remember that it is a sign of their weakness, pettiness, dullness.

10

The Pythagoreans assumed that the sun is motionless and that the earth turns round. What a long time the truth had to wait for recognition !

11

In spite of Epicurus and his exasperation we are forced to admit that anything whatsoever may result from anything whatsoever. Which does not mean, however, that a stone ever turned into bread, or that our visible universe was ever "naturally" formed from nebulous puffs. But from our own minds and our own experience we can deduce nothing that would serve us as a ground for setting even the smallest limit to nature's own arbitrary behaviour. If whatever happens now had chanced to happen quite differently, it would not, therefore, have seemed any the less *natural* to us. In other words, although there may be an element of inevitability in our human judgments concerning the natural phenomena, we have never been able and probably never shall be able to separate the grain of inevitable from the chaff of accidental and casual truth. Moreover, we do not even know which is more essential and important, the inevitable or the casual. Hence we are forced to the conclusion that philosophy must give up her attempt at finding the *veritates aeternae*. The business of philosophy is to teach man to live in uncertainty—man who is supremely afraid of uncertainty, and who is forever hiding himself behind this or the other dogma. More briefly, the business of philosophy is not to reassure people, but to upset them.

12

When man finds in himself a certain defect, of which he can by no means rid himself, there remains but to accept the so-called failing as a natural quality. The more grave and important the defect, the more urgent is the need to ennoble it. From sublime to ridiculous is only one step, and an ineradicable vice in strong men is always rechristened a virtue.

13

On the whole, there is little to choose between metaphysics and positivism. In each there is the same horizon, but the composition and colouring are different. Positivism chooses grey, colourless paint and ordinary composition ; metaphysics prefers brilliant colouring and complicated design, and always carries the vision away into the infinite ; in which trick it often succeeds, owing to its skill in perspective. But the canvas is impervious, there is no melting through it into " the other world." Nevertheless, skilful perspectives are very alluring, so that metaphysicians will still have something to quarrel about with the positivists.

The task of a writer : to go forward and
share his impressions with his reader. In
spite of everything to the contrary, he is
not obliged to *prove* anything. But, because
every step of his progress is dogged by those
police agents, morality, science, logic, and
so forth, he needs always to have ready some
sort of argument with which to frustrate
them. There is no necessity to trouble too
deeply about the quality of the argumentation. Why fret about being "inwardly
right." It is quite enough if the reasoning
which comes handiest will succeed in occupy-
ing those guardians of the verbal highways
whose intention it is to obstruct his passage.

15)

The Secret of Poushkin's "inner harmony."—To Poushkin nothing was hopeless. Nay, he saw hopeful signs in everything. It is agreeable to sin, and it is
just as delightful to repent. It is good to
doubt, but it is still better to believe. It is
jolly "with feet shod in steel" to skate the
ice, it is pleasant to wander about with
gypsies, to pray in church, to quarrel with
a friend, to make peace with an enemy, to
swoon on waves of harmony, to weep over

a passing fancy, to recall the past, to peep into the future. Poushkin could cry hot tears, and he who can weep can hope. "I want to live, so that I may think and suffer," he says; and it seems as if the word "to suffer," which is so beautiful in the poem, just fell in accidentally, because there was no better rhyme in Russian for "to die." The later verses, which are intended to amplify *to think and to suffer*, prove this. Poushkin might repeat the words of the ancient hero: "danger is dangerous to others, but not to me." Therein lies the secret of his harmonious moods.

16

The well-trodden field of contemporary thought should be dug up. Therefore, on every possible occasion, in season and out, the generally-accepted truths must be ridiculed to death, and paradoxes uttered in their place. Then we shall see . . .

17

What is a Weltanschauung, a world-conception, a philosophy? As we all know, Turgenev was a realist, and from the first he tried to portray life truthfully. Although we had had no precise exponents of realism, yet after Poushkin it was impossible for a Russian writer to depart too far from actuality. Even those who did not know what to do with " real life " had to cope with it as best they could. Hence, in order that the picture of life should not prove too depressing, the writer must provide himself in due season with a philosophy. This philosophy still plays the part of the magic wand in literature, enabling the author to turn anything he likes into anything else.

Most of Turgenev's works are curious in respect of philosophy. But most curious is his *Diary of a Superfluous Man*. Turgenev was the first to introduce the term " a superfluous man " into Russian literature. Since then an endless amount has been written about superfluous people, although up till now nothing important has been added to what was already said fifty years ago. There are superfluous people, plenty of them. But what is to be done with them ? No one knows. There remains only to invent philosophies on their behalf. In 1850 Turgenev, then a young man, thus solved the problem. He ends the *Diary* —with a humorous postscript, supposed to have been scribbled by an impertinent reader on the last fly-leaf of the MS.

*This MS. was read, and contents thereof
    disapproved,
by Peter Zudotyeshin.   M.M.M.M.
Dear Sir, Peter Zudotyeshin, My dear Sir.*

It is obvious Turgenev felt that after a
tragedy must follow a farce, and therein
lies the substance of his philosophy. It is
also obvious that in this feeling he has the
whole of European civilisation behind him.
Turgenev was the most educated, the most
cultured of all Russian writers. He spent
nearly all his life abroad, and absorbed into
himself all that European learning could offer.
He knew this, although he never directly
admitted it, owing to an exaggerated
modesty which sometimes irritates us by
its obviousness. He believed profoundly
that only learning, only European science
could open men's eyes to life, and explain
all that needed explanation. According
to this belief he judges even Tolstoy.
"The saddest instance of the lack of real
freedom," the sixty-year-old Turgenev writes
of *War and Peace*, in his literary memoirs :
"the saddest instance of the lack of real
freedom, arising from the lack of real
knowledge, is revealed to us in Leo Tolstoy's
latest work, a work which at the same time,

29

by virtue of its creative, poetic force, ranks almost first among all that has appeared in Russian literature since 1840. No! without culture, without freedom in the widest sense, freedom within oneself, freedom from preconceived ideas, freedom with regard to one's own nation and history, without this, the real artist is unthinkable; without this free air he cannot breathe." Listening to Turgenev one might imagine that he had learned some great secret in the West, a secret which gave him the right to bear himself cheerfully and modestly when other people despaired and lost their heads. . . . A year after the writing of the literary memoirs above quoted, Turgenev happened to be present at the execution of the notorious murderer, Tropman. His impressions are superbly rendered in a long article called "Tropman's Execution." The description produces a soul-shaking effect upon the reader; for I think I shall not exaggerate if I say that the essay is one of the best, at least one of the most vigorous of Turgenev's writings. It is true that Tolstoy describes scenes of slaughter with no less vigour, and therefore the reader need not yield too much to the artist's power. Yet when Turgenev relates that, at the decisive moment, when the executioners like spiders on a fly threw themselves on Tropman and bore him to the ground—" the earth quietly swam away from under my feet "—we are forced to believe him. Men respond only faintly to the horrors that take place around them, except at moments, when the savage, crying incongruity and ghastliness of our condition suddenly reveals itself vivid before our eyes, and we are forced to know what we are. Then the ground slides away from under our feet. But not for long. The horror of the sensation of groundlessness quickly brings man to himself. He must forget everything, he must only get his feet on earth again. In this sense Turgenev proved himself in as risky a state at sixty as he was when, as a young man, he wrote his *Diary of a Superfluous Man*. The description of Tropman's execution ends with these words : " Who can fail to feel that the question of capital punishment is one of the urgent, immediate problems which modern humanity must settle ? I shall be satisfied . . . if my story will provide even a few arguments for those who advocate the abolition, or at least the suppression of the publicity of capital punishments." Again the mountain has brought forth a mouse. After a tragedy, a farce. Philosophy enters into her power, and the earth returns under one's feet.

I emphasise and repeat : Turgenev is not alone responsible for his attitude. With his lips speaks the whole of European civilisation. On principle all insoluble problems are rejected. During her thousand years of experience, the old civilisation has acquired the skill which allows her children to derive satisfaction and benefit out of anything, even the blood of their neighbour. Even the greatest horrors, even crimes are beneficial; properly construed. Turgenev was, as we know, a soft, "humane" man, an undoubted idealist. In his youth he had been through the Hegelian school. And from Hegel he learned what an enormous value education has, and how supremely important it is for an educated man to have a complete and finished—most certainly a "finished" philosophy.

18

To praise oneself is considered improper, immodest ; to praise one's own sect, one's own philosophy, is considered the highest duty. Even the best writers have taken at least as much trouble to glorify their philosophy as to found it, and have always had more success in the former case than in the latter. Their ideas, whether proven or not, are the dearest possession in life to them, in sorrow a consolation, in difficulty a source of counsel. Even death is not terrible to ideas; they will follow man beyond the grave, they are the only imperishable riches. All this the philosophers repeat, very eloquently repeat and reiterate concerning their ideas, not less skilfully than advocates plead their cases on behalf of thieves and swindlers. But nobody has ever yet called a philosopher " a hired conscience," though everybody gives the lawyer this nickname. Why this partiality ?

19

Certain savage tribes believe that their kings need no food, neither to eat nor to drink. As a matter of fact, kings eat and drink, and even relish a good mouthful more than ordinary mortals. So, having no desire, even for the sake of form, to abstain too long, they not infrequently interrupt the long-drawn-out religious ceremonies of their tribes, in order to command refreshment for their frail bodies. But

c

none must witness, or even be aware of this refreshing, and so while he eats the king is hidden within a purple pall. Metaphysicians remind one of these savage kings. They want everyone to believe that empiricism, which means all reality and substantial existence, is nothing to them, they need only pure ideas for their existence. In order to keep up this fiction, they appear before the world invested in a purple veil of fine words. The crowd knows perfectly well that it is all a take-in, but since it likes shows and bright colours, and since also it has no ambition to appear too knowing, it rarely betrays that it has caught the trick of the comedy. On the contrary, it loves to pretend to be fooled, knowing by instinct that actors always do their best when the audience believes implicitly in what happens. Only inexperienced youths and children, unaware of the great importance of the conventional attitide, now and then cry out in indignation and give the lie to the performance: like the child in Andersen's story, who so unexpectedly and inopportunely broke the general, deliberate illusion by calling out—" But the king is naked." Of course everybody knows without telling that the king is naked : that the metaphysicians not only are unable to explain anything, but that hitherto they have not been able to present even a single hypothesis free from contradiction. It is necessary to pretend to believe that kings eat nothing, that philosophers have divined the secrets of the universe, that arbitrary theories are more precious than empirical harvests, and so on. There remains only one difficulty : grown-ups may be won over to the conventional lie, but what about the children ? With them the only remedy is the Pythagorean system of upbringing, so glorified by Hegel. Children must keep silent and not raise their voice until they realise that *some* things may not be talked about. This is our method. With us pupils remain silent, not only for five years, as the Pythagoreans recommended, but for ten or more—until they have learned to speak like their masters. And then they are granted a freedom which is no longer any good to them. Perhaps they had wings, or might have had them, but they have crawled all their life long in imitation of their masters, so how can they now dream of flight ? To a well-informed man, who has studied much, the very thought of the possibility of tearing

himself away from the earth, even for a
moment, is horrifying: as if he knew
beforehand what the result would be.

(20)

The best, the most effective way of
convincing a reader is to begin one's argument with inoffensive, commonplace assertions. When suspicion has been sufficiently
lulled, and a certainty has been begot that
what follows will be a confirmation of the
readers own accepted views—then has the
moment arrived to speak one's mind openly,
but still in the same easy tone, as if there
were no break in the flow of truisms. The
logical connection is unimportant. Consequence of manner and intonation is much
more impressive than consequence of ideas.
The thing to do is to go on, in the same
suave tone, from uttering a series of banalities to expressing a new and dangerous
thought, without any break. If you succeed in this, the business is done. The
reader will not forget—the new words will
plague and torment him until he has
accepted them.

The habit of logical thinking kills imagination. Man is convinced that the only way to truth is through logic, and that any departure from this way leads to error and absurdity. The nearer we approach the ultimate questions of existence, in our departure from logicality, the more deadly becomes the state of error we fall into. The Ariadne ball has become all unwound long ago, and man is at the end of the tether. But he does not know, he holds the end of the thread firmly, and marks time with energy on the same spot, imagining his progress, and little realising the ridiculous situation into which he has fallen. How should he realise, considering the innumerable precautions he has taken to prevent himself from losing the logical way? He had better have stayed at home. Once he set out, once he decided to be a Theseus and kill the Minotaur, he should have given himself up, forfeited the old attachment, and been ready *never to escape from the labyrinth*. True, he would have risked losing Ariadne: and this is why long journeys should be undertaken only after family connections have become a burden. Such being the case, a man deliberately cuts the

37

thread which binds him to hearth and home, so that he may have a legitimate excuse to his conscience for not going back. Philosophy must have nothing in common with logic; philosophy is an art which aims at breaking the logical continuity of argument and bringing man out on the shoreless sea of imagination, the fantastic tides where everything is equally possible and impossible. Certainly it is difficult, given sedentary habits of life, to be a good philosopher. The fact that the fate of philosophy has ever lain in the hands of professors can only be explained by the reluctance of the envious gods to give omniscience to mortals. Whilst stay-at-home persons are searching for truth, the apple will stay on the tree. The business must be undertaken by homeless adventurers, born nomads, to whom *ubi bene ibi patria*. It seems to me that but for his family and his domesticity, Count Tolstoy, who lives to such a ripe old age, might have told us a great many important and interesting things. . . . Or, perhaps, had he not married, like Nietszche he would have gone mad. "If you turn to the right, you will marry, if to the left, you will be killed." A true philosopher never chooses the middle course;

he needs no riches, he does not know what to do with money. But whether he turns to the right or to the left, nothing pleasant awaits him.

22

Scratch a Russian and you will find a Tartar. Culture is an age-long development, and sudden grafting of it upon a race rarely succeeds. To us in Russia, civilisation came suddenly, whilst we were still savages. At once she took upon herself the responsibilities of a tamer of wild animals, first working with decoys and baits, and later, when she felt her power, with threats. We quickly submitted. In a short time we were swallowing in enormous doses those poisons which Europe had been gradually accustoming herself to, gradually assimilating through centuries. Thanks to which, the transplanting of civilisation into Russia turns out to be no mild affair. A Russian had only to catch a whiff of European atmosphere, and his head began to swim. He interpreted in his own way, savage-like, whatever he heard of western success. Hearing about railways, agricultural machines, schools, municipalities, his imagination painted miracles: universal happiness, boundless freedom, paradise, wings, etc. And the more impossible his dreams, the more eager he was to believe them real. How disillusioned with Europe the westerner *Herzen* became, after living for years on end abroad! Yet, with all his acuteness, it did not occur to him that Europe was not in the least to blame for his disillusionment. Europe had dropped miracles ages ago; she contented herself with ideals. It is we in Russia who will go on confusing miracles with ideals, as if the two were identical, whereas they have nothing to do with each other. As a matter of fact, just because Europe had ceased to believe in miracles, and realised that all human problems resolve down to mere arrangements here on earth, ideas and ideals had been invented. But the Russian bear crept out of his hole and strolled to Europe for the elixir of life, the flying carpet, the seven-leagued shoes, and so on, thinking in all his naïveté that railways and electricity were signs which clearly proved that the old nurse never told a lie in her fairy tales. . . . All this happened just at the moment when Europe had finally made away with alchemy and astrology, and started on the positive researches resulting in chemistry and astronomy.

The first assumption of all metaphysics is, that by dialectic development of any concept a whole system can be evolved. Of course the initial concept, the *a priori*, is generally unsound, so there is no need to mention the deductions. But since it is very difficult in the realm of abstract thought to distinguish a lie from truth, metaphysical systems often have a very convincing appearance. The chief defect only appears incidentally, when the taste for dialectic play becomes blunted in man, as it did in Turgenev towards the end of his life, so that he realises the uselessness of philosophical systems. It is related that a famous mathematician, after hearing a musical symphony to the end, inquired, "What does it prove?" Of course, it proves nothing, except that the mathematician had no taste for music. And to him who has no taste for dialectics, metaphysics can prove nothing, either. Therefore, those who are interested in the success of metaphysics must always encourage the opinion that a taste for dialectics is a high distinction in a man, proving the loftiness of his soul.

Man is used to having convictions, so there we are. We can none of us do without our hangers-on, though we despise them at the bottom of our souls.

Socrates and Plato tried to determine under the shifting change of appearance the immutable, unchanging reality. In the Platonic " ideas " the attempt was incarnated. The visible reality, never true to itself, assuming numberless varying forms, this is not the genuine reality. That which is real must be constant. Hence the ideas of objects are real, and the objects themselves are fictitious. Thus the root of the Platonic philosophy appears to be a fundamental defect in human reasoning—a defect regarded as the highest merit. It is difficult for the philosopher to get a good grasp of this agitated, capricious life, and so he decides that it is not life at all, but a figment. Dialectics is supreme only over general concepts—and the general concepts are promoted to an ideal. Since Plato and Socrates, only such philosophers have succeeded largely who have taught that the unchangeable is preferable to the changeable, the eternal to the temporal. The ordinary individual, who lives unconsciously, never reckoning his spiritual credit against his spiritual debit, naturally regards the philosopher as his legitimate book-keeper, keeper of the soul's accounts. Already in Greece the Athenian youth watched with passionate interest the dexterity which Socrates displayed in his endeavour to restore by means of dialectics the lost " ultimate foundations " of human conduct. Now in book-keeping, as we are aware, not a single farthing must disappear untraceably. Socrates was trying to come up to expectations. The balance between man's spiritual assets and liabilities was with him ideally established. Perhaps in this lies the secret of that strange attraction he exerted even over such volatile and unsteady natures as that of Alcibiades, drawing the young men to him so that they were attached to him with all their soul. Alcibiades had long since lost all count of his spiritual estate, and therefore from time to time he had need to recourse to Socrates, who by speeches and dissertations could bring order into chaos and harmony into the spiritual confusion of his young friend. Alcibiades turned to Socrates to be relieved. Of

43

course, he sought relief in order that he might begin again his riotous living : rest is so sweet to a tired man. But to conclude that because Alcibiades exhausted himself, and because rest is sweet, therefore all men must rest, this is absurd. Yet Socrates dictated this conclusion, in all his ideas. He wished that all men should rest, rest through eternity, that they should see their highest fulfilment in this resting. It is easier to judge of Socrates since we have Count Tolstoy with us. Probably the physiognomist Topir would say of Tolstoy as he said of Socrates, that there are many evil propensities lurking in him. Topir is not here to speak, but Tolstoy has told us himself how wicked he found his own nature, how he had to struggle with it. Tolstoy is not naturally over-courageous ; by long effort he has trained himself to be bold. How afraid of death he was in his youth And how cleverly he could conceal that fear. Later on, in mature age, it was still the fear of death which inspired him to write his confession. He was conquering that fear, and with it all other fears. For he felt that, since fear is very difficult to master in oneself, man must be a much higher being when he has learned not to be afraid

44

any more. Meanwhile, who knows ? Perhaps " cowardice," that miserable, despicable, much-abused weakness of the underworld, is not such a vice after all. Perhaps it is even a virtue. Think of Dostoevsky and his heroes, think of Hamlet. If the underworld man in us were afraid of nothing, if Hamlet was naturally a gladiator, then we should have neither tragic poetry nor philosophy. It is a platitude, that fear of death has been the inspiration of philosophers. Numberless quotations could be drawn from ancient and modern writers, if they were necessary. Maybe the poetic daimon of Socrates, which made him wise, was only fear personified. Or perhaps it was his dark dreams. That which troubled him by day did not quit him by night. Even after the sentence of death Socrates dreamed that he ought to engage in the arts, so in order not to provoke the gods he began to compose verses, at the age of seventy. Tolstoy also at the age of fifty began to perform good deeds, to which performance he had previously given not the slightest attention. If it were our custom nowadays to express ourselves mythologically, we should no doubt hear Tolstoy telling us about his daimon or his dreams. Instead he squares his accounts with science and morality, in place of gods or demons. Many a present-day Alcibiades, who laves all the week in the muddy waters of life, comes on Sundays to cleanse himself in the pure stream of Tolstoyian ideas. Book-keeping is satisfied with this modest success, and assumes that if it commands universal attention one day in the week, then obviously it is the sum and essence of life, beyond which man needs nothing. On the same grounds the keepers of public baths could argue that, since so many people come to them on Saturdays, therefore cleanliness is the highest ambition of man, and during the week no one should stir at all, lest he sweat or soil himself.

26

In an old French writer, a contemporary of Pascal, I came across the following remarkable words : " L'homme est si misérable que *l'inconstance avec laquelle il abandonne ses desseins est, en quelque sorte, sa plus grande vertu ;* parce qu'il temoigne par là qu'il y a encore en lui quelque reste de grandeur qui le porte à se dégouter de choses qui ne méritent pas son amour et son estime." What a long way modern

thought has travelled from even the possibility of such an assumption. To consider
inconstancy the finest human virtue! Surely
in order to get somewhere in life it is necessary to give the whole self, one's whole
energy to the service of some one particular
purpose. In order to be a *virtuoso*, a master
of one's art and one's instrument, it is
necessary with a truly angelic or asinine
patience to try over and over again, dozens,
hundreds, thousands of times, different
ways of expressing one's ideas or moods,
sparing neither labour, nor time, nor health.
Everything else must take a second place.
The first must be occupied by " the Art."
Goncharov, in his novel *Obryv*, cleverly
relates how a 'cellist struggled all day, like
a fish against the ice, sawing and sawing
away, so that later on, in the evening, he
might play super-excellently well. And
that is the general idea. Objectionable,
tedious, irritating labour,—this is the condition of genius, which no doubt explains the
reason why men so rarely achieve anything.
Genius must submit to cultivate an ass
within itself—the condition being so humiliating that man will seldom take up the job.
The majority prefer talent, that medium
which lies between genius and mediocrity.

47

And many a time, towards the end of life, does the genius repent of his choice. "It would be better not to startle the world, but to live at one with it," says Ibsen in his last drama. Genius is a wretched, blind maniac, whose eccentricities are condoned because of what is got from him. And still we all bow to persevering talent, to the only god in whom we moderns believe, and the eulogy of inconstancy will awake very little sympathy in our hearts. Probably we shall not even regard it seriously.

27

We very often express in a categorical form a judgment of which we do not feel assured, we even lay stress on its absolute validity. We want to see what opposition it will arouse, and this can be achieved only by stating our assumption not as a tentative suggestion, which no one will consider, but as an irrefutable, all-important truth. The greater the value an assumption has for us, the more carefully do we conceal any suggestion of its improbability.

28

Literature deals with the most difficult and important problems of existence, and, therefore, littérateurs consider themselves the most important of people. A bank clerk, who is always handing money out, might just as well consider himself a millionaire. The high estimate placed upon unexplained, unsolved questions ought really to discredit writers in our eyes. And yet these literary men are so clever, so cunning at stating their own case and revealing the high importance of their mission, that in the long run they convince everybody, themselves most of all. This last event is surely owing to their own limited intelligence. The Romans augurs had subtler, more versatile minds. In order to deceive others, they had no need to deceive themselves. In their own set they were not afraid to talk about their secrets, even to make fun of them, being fully confident that they could easily vindicate themselves before outsiders, in case of necessity, and pull a solemn face befitting the occasion. But our writers of to-day, before they can lay their improbable assertions before the public, must inevitably try to be convinced in their own minds. Otherwise they cannot begin.

29

" The writer is writing away, the reader
is reading away "—the writer doesn't care
what the reader is after, the reader doesn't
care what the writer is about. Such a
state of things hurt Schedrin very much.
He would have liked it different ; no sooner
has the writer said a word, than the reader
at once scales the wall. This was his
ideal. But the reader is by no means so
naïve as all that. He prefers to rest easy,
and insists that the writer shall climb the
wall for him. So those authors succeed
with the public who write " with their
heart's blood." Conventional tournaments,
even the most brilliant, do not attract the
masses any more than the connoisseurs.
People rush to see a fight of gladiators,
where awaits them a scent of real, hot,
smoking blood, where they are going to
see real, not pretended victims.

Thus many writers, like gladiators, shed
their blood to gratify that modern Caesar,
the mob. " *Salve, Caesar, morituri te
salutant !* "

30

Anton Tchekov tells the truth neither
out of love or respect for the truth, nor yet
because, in the Kantian manner, a high

50

duty bids him never to tell a lie, even to escape death. Neither has he the impulse which so often pushes young and fiery souls into rashness : that desire to stand erect, to keep the head high. On the contrary, Tchekhov always walks with a stoop, his head bent down, never fixing his eyes on the heavens, since he will read no signs there. If he tells the truth, it is because the most reeking lie no longer intoxicates him, even though he swallow it not in the modest doses that idealism offers, but in immoderate quantities, thousand-gallon-barrel gulps. He would taste the bitterness, but it would not make his head turn, as it does Schiller's, or Dostoevsky's, or even Socrates', whose head, as we know, could stand any quantity of wine, but went spinning with the most commonplace lie.

31

Noblesse Oblige.—The moment of obligation, compulsion, duty, that moment described by Kant as the essential, almost the only predicate of moral concepts, serves chiefly to indicate that Kant was modest in himself and in his attitude towards all whom he addressed, perceiving in all men beings subject to the ennobling effect of morality. *Noblesse oblige* is a motto not for the aristocracy, which recognises in its privileges its own instant duties, but for the self-made, wealthy *parvenues* who pant for an illustrious title. They have been accustomed to telling lies, to playing poltroon, swindling, and meanness, and the necessity for speaking the truth impartially, for bravely facing danger, for freely giving of their fortunes scares them beyond measure. Therefore it is necessary that they should repeat it to themselves and to their children, in whose veins the lying, sneaking blood still runs, hourly, lest they forget : " You must not tell lies, you must be open, magnanimous." It is silly, it is incomprehensible—but " *noblesse oblige.*"

32

Homo homini lupus is one of the most steadfast maxims of eternal morality. In each of our neighbours we fear a wolf. " This fellow is evil-minded, if he is not restrained by law he will ruin us," so we think every time a man gets out of the rut of sanctified tradition.

The fear is just. We are so poor, so weak, so easily ruined and destroyed ! How can we help being afraid ! And yet, behind danger and menace there is usually hidden something significant, which merits our close and sympathetic attention. But fear's eyes are big. We see danger, danger only, we build up a fabric of morality inside which as in a fortress we sit out of danger all our lives. Only poets have undertaken to praise dangerous people—Don Juans, Fausts, Tannhaüsers. But nobody takes the poets seriously. Common-sense values a commercial-traveller or a don much more highly than a Byron, a Goethe, or a Molière.

33

The possibilities which open out before mankind are sufficiently limited. It is impossible to see everything, impossible to know everything, impossible to rise too high above the earth, impossible to penetrate too deeply down. What has been is hidden away, what will be we cannot anticipate, and we know for certain that we shall never grow wings. Regularity, immutably regular succession of phenomena puts a term to our efforts, drives us into a regular, narrow, hard-beaten road of everyday life. But even on this road we may not wander from side to side. We must watch our feet, consider each step, since the moment we are off our guard disaster is upon us. Another life is conceivable, however: life in which the word disaster does not exist, where responsibility for one's actions, even if it be not completely abolished, at least has not such a deadly and accidental weight, and where, on the other hand, there is no "regularity," but rather an infinite number of possibilities. In such a life the sense of fear—most disgraceful to us—disappears. There the virtues are not the same as ours. Fearlessness in face of danger, liberality, even lavishness are considered virtues with us, but they are respected without any grounds. Socrates was quite right when he argued that not all courage, but only the courage which measures beforehand the risks and the chances of victory, is fully justifiable. To the same extent those economical, careful people who condemn lavishness are in the right. Fearlessness and lavishness do not suit mortal men, rather it becomes them to tremble and to count every penny, seeing what a state of poverty and impotence they exist in. That is why these two virtues are so rarely met with, and when they are met, why they arouse such superstitious reverence in the crowd. " This man fears nothing and spares nothing : he is probably not a man, but a demi-god, perhaps even a god." Socrates did not believe in gods, so he wanted to justify virtue by reason. Kant also did not believe in God, and therefore he derived his morals from " Law." But if there is God, and all men are the children of God, then we should be afraid of nothing and spare nothing. And then the man who madly dissipates his own life and fortunes, and the lives and fortunes of others, is more right than the calculating philosophers who vainly seek to regulate mankind on earth.

34

Moral people are the most revengeful of mankind, they employ their morality as the best and most subtle weapon of vengeance. They are not satisfied with simply despising and condemning their neighbour *themselves*, they want the condemnation to be universal and supreme : that is, that all men should rise as one against the condemned, *and that even the offender's own conscience shall be against him*. Then only are they fully satisfied and reassured. Nothing on earth but morality could lead to such wonderful results.

35

Inveterate wickedness.—Heretics were often most bitterly persecuted for their least digression from accepted belief. It was just their obstinacy in trifles that irritated the righteous to madness. "Why can they not yield on so trifling a matter? They cannot possibly have serious cause for opposition. They only want to grieve us, to spite us." So the hatred mounted up, piles of faggots and torture machines appeared against obdurate wickedness.

36

I do not know where I came across the remark, whether in Tolstoy or Turgenev, that those who have been subjected to trial in the courts of justice always acquire a particularly noble expression of face. Although logic does so earnestly recommend caution in the forming of contradictory conclusions, come what may I shall for once risk a deduction: a noble expression of face is a sign that a man has been under trial—but certainly not a trial for political crime—for theft or bribe-taking.

37

The most important and significant revelations come into the world naked, without a wordy garment. To find words for them is a delicate, difficult business, a whole art. Stupidities and banalities, on the contrary, appear at once in ready-made apparel, gaudy even if shabby. So that they are ready straight away to be presented to the public.

38

A strange impatience has taken possession of Russian writers lately. They are all running a race after the "ultimate words." They have no doubt that the ultimate words will be attained. The question is, who will lay hold of them first.

39

The appearance of Socrates on the philosophic horizon is hailed by historians as the greatest event. Morals were beginning to work loose, Athens was threatened with ruin. Socrates' mission was to put an end to the violent oscillation in moral judgments which extreme individualism on the one hand and the relativism of the sophists on the other had set up. The great teacher did all he could. He gave up his usual occupations and his family life, he took no thought for the morrow, he taught, taught, taught—simple people or eminent, wise or foolish, ignorant or learned. Notwithstanding, he did not save the country. Under Pericles, Athens flourished without wisdom, or at least independently of Socratic wisdom. After Pericles, in spite of the fact that the Socratic teaching found such a genius as Plato to continue it, Athens steadily declined, and Aristotle is already master to the son of Philip of Macedon. Whence it is obvious that the wisdom of Socrates had not saved the country, and as this had been its chief object, it had failed in its object, and therefore was not worthy of the exaggerated respect it received. It is necessary to find some justification for philosophy other than country-saving. This would be the easiest thing in the world. But altogether we must give up the favourite device of the philosophers, of looking to find in the well-being of society the *raison d'être* of philosophy. At the best, the trick was a risky one. As a rule, wisdom goes one way, society the other. They are artificially connected. It is public orators who have trained both the philosophers and the masses to regard as worthy of attention only those considerations which have absolutely everything on their side : social utility, morality, even metaphysical wisdom. . . . Why so much ? Is it not sufficient if some new project will prove useful ? Why try to get the sanction of morality and metaphysics ? Nay, once the laws of morality are autonomous, and once ideas are allowed to stand above the empirical needs of mankind, it is impossible to balance ideas and morality with social requirements, or even with the salvation of the country from ruin. *Pereat mundus, fiat philosophia.* If Athens was ruined because of philosophy, philosophy is not impugned. So the autonomous thinker should hold. But *de facto*, a thinker does not like quarrelling with his country.

40

When a writer has to express an idea whose foundation he has not been able to establish, and which yet is dear to his heart, so that he earnestly wishes to secure its general acceptance, as a rule he interrupts his exposition, as if to take breath, and makes a small, or at times a serious digression, during which he proves the invalidity of this or that proposition, often without any reference to his real theme. Having triumphantly exposed one or more absurdities, and thus acquired the aplomb of a solid expert, he returns to his proper task, calculating that now he will inspire his reader with greater confidence. His calculation is perfectly justified. The reader is afraid to attack such a skilled dialectician, and prefers to agree rather than to risk himself in argument. Not even the greatest intellects, particularly in philosophy, disdain such stratagems. The idealists, for example, before expounding their theories, turn and rend materialism. The materialists, we remember, at one time did the same with the idealists, and achieved a vast success.

41

Theories of sequence and consequence are binding only upon the disciples, not upon the masters. Fathers of great ideas tend to be very careless about their progeny, giving very little heed to their future career. The offspring of one and the same philosopher frequently bear such small resemblance to one another, that it is impossible to discern the family connection. Conscientious disciples, wasting away under the arduous effort to discover that which does not exist, are brought to despair of their task. Having got an inkling of the truth concerning their difficulty, they give up the job for ever, they cease their attempt at reconciling glaring contradictions. But then they only insist the harder upon the necessity for studying the philosophers, studying them minutely, circumstantially, historically, philologically even. So the history of philosophy is born, which now is taking the place of philosophy. Certainly the history of philosophy may be an exact science, since by means of historical research it is often possible to decide what exactly a certain philosopher did mean, and in what sense he employed his peculiar terms. And seeing that there have been a fair number of philosophers, the business of clearing them all up is a respectable undertaking, and deserves the name of a science. For a good translation or a commentary on the chief works of Kant a man may be given the degree of doctor of philosophy, and henceforth recognised as one who is initiated in the profundities of the secrets of the universe. Then why ever should anybody think out new systems—or even write them ?

The raptures of creative activity !—empty
words, invented by men who never had an
opportunity of judging from their own
experience, but who derive their conclusion
syllogistically : " if a creation gives us such
delight, what must the creator himself
experience ! " Usually the creator feels only
vexations. Every creation is created out of
the Void. At the best, the maker finds
himself confronted with a formless, meaningless, usually obstinate and stiff matter,
which yields reluctantly to form. And he
does not know how to begin. Every time a
new thought is gendered, so often must that
new thought, which for the moment seems so
brilliant and fascinating, be thrown aside as
worthless. Creative activity is a continual
progression from failure to failure, and the
condition of the creator is usually one of
uncertainty, mistrust, and shattered nerves.
The more serious and original the task which
a man sets himself, the more tormenting
is the self-misgiving. For this reason even
men of genius cannot keep up the creative
activity to the last. As soon as they have
acquired their technique, they begin to
repeat themselves, well aware that the
public willingly endures the monotony of a

favourite, even finds virtue in it. Every connoisseur of art is satisfied if he recognises in a new work the accepted "manner" of the artist. Few realise that the acquiring of a manner is the beginning of the end. Artists realise well enough, and would be glad to be rid of their manner, which seems to them a hackneyed affair. But this requires too great a strain on their powers, new torments, doubts, new groping. He who has once been through the creative raptures is not easily tempted to try again. He prefers to turn out work according to the pattern he has evolved, calmly and securely, assured of his results. Fortunately no one except himself knows that he is not any longer a creator. What a lot of secrets there are in the world, and how easy it is to keep one's secret safe from indiscreet glances !

43

A writer works himself up to a pitch of ecstasy, otherwise he does not take up his pen. But ecstasy is not so easily distinguished from other kinds of excitement. And as a writer is always in haste to write, he has rarely the patience to wait, but at the first promptings of animation begins to pour himself forth. So in the name of ecstasy we are offered such quantities of banal, by no means ecstatic effusions. Particularly easy it is to confound with ecstasy that very common sort of spring-time liveliness which in our language is well-named calf-rapture. And calf-rapture is much more acceptable to the public than true inspiration or genuine transport. It is easier, more familiar.

44

A school axiom : logical scepticism refutes itself, since the denial of the possibility of positive knowledge is already an affirmation. But, in the first place, scepticism is not bound to be logical, for it has no desire whatever to gratify that dogma which raises logic to the position of law. Secondly, where is the philosophic theory which, if carried to its extreme, would not destroy itself ? Therefore, why is more demanded from scepticism than from other systems ? especially from scepticism, which honestly avows that it cannot give that which all other theories claim to give.

45

The Aristotelian logic, which forms the chief component in modern logic, arose, as we know, as a result of the permanent controversies which were such sport to the

Greeks. In order to argue, it is indeed necessary to have a common ground; in other words, to agree about the rules of the game. But in our day dialectic tournaments, like all other bouts of contention, no longer attract people. Thus logic may be relegated to the background.

46

In Gogol's *Portrait*, the artist despairs at the thought that he has sacrificed art for the sake of "life." In Ibsen's drama, *When We Dead Awaken*, there is also an artist, who has become world-famous, and who repents that he has sacrificed his life— to art. Now, choose—which of the two ways of repentance do you prefer ?

47

Man is often quite indifferent to success whilst he has it. But once he loses his power over people, he begins to fret. And —vice versa.

48

Turgenev's Insarov strikes the imagination of Elena because he is a man preparing for battle. She prefers him to Shubin the painter, or to Berseniev the savant. Since

ancient days women have looked with favour
on warriors rather than on peaceful men.
Had Turgenev invested that idea with less
glamour, he would probably not have become
the ideal of the young. Who does not get a
thrill from Elena and her elect ? Who has not
felt the fascination of Turgenev's women!
And yet all of them give themselves to the
strong male. With such " superior people," as
with beasts, the males fight with each other,
the woman looks on, and when it is over, she
submits herself the slave of the conqueror.

49

A caterpillar is transformed into a
chrysalis, and for a long time lives in a
warm, quiet little world. Perhaps if it had
human consciousness it would declare that
that world was the best, perhaps the only one
possible to live in. But there comes a time
when some unknown influence causes the
little creature to begin the work of destruction. If other caterpillars could see it how
horrified they would be, revolted to the
bottom of their soul by the awful work in
which the insurgent is engaged. They
would call it immoral, godless, they would
begin to talk about pessimism, scepticism, and
so on. To destroy what has cost such labour

to construct! Why, what is wrong with this complete, cosy, comfortable little world? To keep it intact they call to their aid sacred morality and the idealistic theory of knowledge. Nobody cares that the caterpillar has grown wings, that when it has nibbled its old nest away it will fly out into space—nobody gives a thought to this.

Wings—that is mysticism; self-nibbling—this is actuality. Those who are engaged in such actuality deserve torture and execution. And there are plenty of prisons and voluntary hangmen on the bright earth. The majority of books are prisons, and great authors are not bad hangmen.

(50)

Nietzsche and Dostoevsky seem to be typical "inverted simulators," if one may use the expression. They imitated spiritual sanity, although they were spiritually insane. They knew their morbidity well enough, but they exhibited their disease only to that extent where freakishness passes for originality. With the sensitiveness peculiar to all who are in constant danger, they never went beyond the limits. The axe of the guillotine of public opinion hung over them: one awkward move, and the execution

67

automatically takes place. But they knew
how to avoid unwarrantable moves.

51

The so-called ultimate questions troubled
mankind in the world's dawn as badly as they
trouble us now. Adam and Eve wanted
"to know," and they plucked the fruit at
their risk. Cain, whose sacrifice did not
please God, raised his hand against his
brother : and it seemed to him he committed
murder in the name of justice, in vindication
of his own injured rights. Nobody has ever
been able to understand why God preferred
Abel's sacrifice to that of Cain. In our own
day Sallieri repeats Cain's vengeance and
poisons his friend and benefactor Mozzart,
according to the poem of Poushkin. "All
say, there is no justice on earth ; but there is
no justice up above : this is as clear to me as
a simple scale of music." No man on earth
can fail to recognise in these words his own
tormenting doubts. The outcome is creative
tragedy, which for some mysterious reason
has been considered up till now as the highest
form of human creation. Everything is
being unriddled and explained. If we compare our knowledge with that of the ancients,
we appear very wise. But we are no nearer

68

to solving the riddle of eternal justice than
Cain was. Progress, civilisation, all the
conquests of the human mind have brought
us nothing new here. Like our ancestors,
we stand still with fright and perplexity
before ugliness, disease, misery, senility,
death. All that the wise men have been
able to do so far is to turn the earthly horrors
into problems. We are told that perhaps all
that is horrible only *appears* horrible, that
perhaps at the end of the long journey something new awaits us. Perhaps! But the
modern educated man, with the wisdom of
all the centuries of mankind at his command,
knows no more about it than the old singer
who solved universal problems at his own
risk. We, the children of a moribund
civilisation, we, old men from our birth, in
this respect are as young as the first man.

52

They say it is impossible to set a bound
between the "I" and society. *Naïveté!*
Crusoes are to be found not only on desert
islands. They are there, in populous cities.
It is true they are not clad in skins, they
have no dark Fridays in attendance, and so
nobody recognises them. But surely Friday
and a fur jacket do not make a Crusoe.

69

Loneliness, desertion, a boundless, shoreless sea, on which no sail has risen for tens of years,—do not many of our contemporaries live in such a circumstance ? And are they not Crusoes, to whom the rest of people have become a vague reminiscence, barely distinguishable from a dream ?

53

To be irremediably unhappy—this is shameful. An irremediably unhappy person is outside the laws of the earth. Any connection between him and society is severed finally. And since, sooner or later, every individual is doomed to irremediable unhappiness, *the last word of philosophy is loneliness.*

54

"It is better to be an unhappy man, than a happy pig." The utilitarians hoped by this golden bridge to get over the chasm which separates them from the promised land of the ideal. But psychology stepped in and rudely interrupted : *There are no unhappy people, the unhappy ones are all pigs.* Dostoevsky's philosopher of the underworld, Raskolnikov, also Hamlet, and suchlike, are not simply unhappy men whose fate might be esteemed, or even preferred before some happy fates; they are simply unhappy swine. And they themselves are principally aware of it . . . . He that hath ears to hear, let him hear.

55

If you want people to envy you your sorrow or your shame, look as if you were proud of it. If you have only enough of the actor in you, rest assured, you will become the hero of the day. Since the parable of the Pharisee and the publican was uttered, what a lot of people who could not fulfil their sacred duties pretended to be publicans and sinners, and so aroused sympathy, even envy.

56

Philosophers dearly love to call their utterances " truths," since in that guise they become binding upon us all. But each philosopher invents his own truths. Which means that he asks his pupils to deceive themselves in the way he shows, but that he reserves for himself the option of deceiving himself in his own way. Why ? Why not allow everyone to deceive himself just as he likes ?

57

When Xanthippe poured slops over Socrates, as he returned from his philosophical occupations, tradition says that he observed : " After a storm there is always rain." Would it not be more worthy (not of the philosopher, but of philosophy) to say : After one's philosophical exercise, one feels as if one had had slops emptied over one's head. And therefore Xanthippe did but give outward expression to what had taken place in Socrates' soul. Symbols are not always beautiful.

58

From the notes of an underworld man— " I read little, I write little, and, it seems to me, I think little. He who is ill-disposed towards me will say that this shows a great defect in my character, perhaps he will call me lazy, an Oblomov, and will repeat the copy-book maxim that idleness is the mother of all the vices. A friend, on the other hand, will say it is only a temporary state, that perhaps I am not quite well— in short, he will find random excuses for me, more with the idea of consoling me than of speaking the truth. But for my part, I say let us wait. If it turns out at the end

of my life that I have 'done' not less
than others—why, then—it will mean that
idleness may be a virtue."

59

Börne, a contemporary of Heine, was
very much offended when his enemies
insisted on explaining his misanthropic out-
pourings as the result of a stomach and
liver disease. It seemed to him much
nobler and loftier to be indignant and
angry because of the triumph of evil on
earth, than because of the disorders of
his own physical organs. Sentimentality
apart—was he right, and is it really nobler ?

60

A real writer *disdains* to repeat from
hearsay events which he has not witnessed.
It seems to him tedious and humiliating
to tell "in his own words," like a schoolboy, things which he has fished out of
another man's books. But there—how can
we expect him to stoop to such insignificance !

61

Whilst conscience stands between the
educated and the lower classes, as the only
possible mediator, there can be no hope for

73

mutual understanding. Conscience demands sacrifices, nothing but sacrifices. It says to the educated man: "You are happy, well-off, learned—the people are poor, unhappy, ignorant; renounce therefore your well-being, or else soothe your conscience with suave speeches." Only he who has nothing to sacrifice, nothing to lose, having lost everything, can hope to approach the people as an equal.

This is why Dostoevsky and Nietzsche were not afraid to speak in their own name, and did not feel compelled either to stretch up or to stoop down in order to be on a level with men.

62

Not to know what you want is considered a shameful weakness. To confess it is to lose for ever not only the reputation of a writer, but even of a man. None the less, "conscience" demands such a confession. True, in this case as in most others the demands of conscience are satisfied only when they incur no very dire consequences. Leaving aside the fact that people are no longer terrified of the once-so-terrible public opinion (the public has been tamed, it listens with reverence to what is told to it, and never dares judge)—the admission "I do not know myself what I want" seems to offer a guarantee of something important. Those who know what they want generally want trifles, and attain to inglorious ends: riches, fame, or at the best, progress or a philosophy of their own. Even now it is sometimes not a sin to laugh at such wonders, and may-be the time is coming when a rehabilitated Hamlet will announce, not with shame but with pride: "I don't in the least know what I want." And the crowd will applaud him, for the crowd always applauds heroes and proud men.

63

Fear of death is explained conclusively by the desire for self-preservation. But at that rate the fear should disappear in old and sick people, who ought by nature to look with indifference on death. Whereas the horror of death is present in all living things. Does not this suggest that there is still some other reason for the dread, and that even where the pangs of horror cannot save a man from his end, still it is a necessary and purposeful anguish? The natural-scientific explanation here, as usual, stops halfway, and fails to lead the human mind to the promised goal.

64

Moral indignation is only a refined form of ancient vengeance. Once anger spoke with daggers, now words will do. And happy is the man who, loving and thirsting to chastise his offender, yet is appeased when the offence is punished. On account of the gratification it offers to the passions, morality, which has replaced bloody chastisement, will not easily lose its charm. But there are offences, deep, unforgettable offences, inflicted not by people, but by "laws of nature." How are we to settle these? Here neither dagger nor indignant word will serve. Therefore, for him who has once run foul of the laws of nature morality sinks, for ever or for a time, into subsidiary importance.

65

Fatalism frightens people particularly in that form which holds it just to say, of anything that happens, or has happened, or will happen: be it so! How can one acquiesce in the actuality of life, when it contains so many horrors? But *amor fati* does not imply eternal acquiescence in actuality. It is only a truce, for a more or less lasting period. Time is needed in which to estimate the forces and intentions of the enemy. Under the mask of friendship the old enmity persists, and an awful revenge is in preparation.

66

In the " ultimate questions of life " we are not a bit nearer the truth than our ancestors were. Everybody knows it, and yet so many go on talking about infinity, without any hope of ever saying anything. It is evident that a result—in the usual acceptance of the word—is not necessary. In the very last resort we trust to instinct, even in the field of philosophy, where reason is supposed to reign supreme, uttering its eternal " Why ? " " Why ? " laughs at all possible "becauses." Instinct, however, does not mock. It simply ignores the whys, and leads us by impossible ways to ends that our divine reason would hold absurd, if it could only see them in time. But reason is a laggard, without much foresight, and therefore, when we have run up to an unexpected conclusion, nothing remains but for reason to accept : or even to justify, to exalt the new event. And therefore,—" reality is reasonable," say the philosophers : reasonable, not only when they draw their philosophic salaries, as the socialists, and with them our philosopher Vladimir Sóloviov, explain; but still reasonable even when philosophers have their maintenance taken away from them. Nay, in the latter case, particularly in the latter case, in spite of the socialists and Vl. Soloviov, reality shows herself most reasonable. A philosopher persecuted, downtrodden, hungry, cold, receiving no salary, is nearly always an extreme fatalist— although this, of course, by no means hinders him from abusing the existing order. Theories of sequence and consequence, as we already know, are binding only upon disciples, whose single virtue lies in their scrupulous, logical developing of the master's idea. But masters themselves *invent* ideas, and, therefore, have the right to substitute one for another. The sovereign power which proclaims a law has the same power to abolish it. But the duty of the subordinate consists in the praise, in the consequential interpretation and the strict observance of the dictates of the higher will.

The Pharisee in the parable fulfilled all that religion demanded of him : kept his fasts, paid his tithes, etc. Had he a right to be pleased with his own piety, and to despise the erring publican ? Everybody thought so, including the Pharisee himself. *The judgment of Christ came as the greatest surprise to him.* He had a clear conscience. He did not merely pretend before others to be righteous, he himself believed in his own righteousness. And suddenly he turns out guilty, awfully guilty. But if the conscience of a righteous man does not help him to distinguish between good and evil, how is he to avoid sin ? What does Kant's moral law mean, that law which was as consoling as the starry sky ? Kant lived his life in profound peace of soul, he met his death quietly, in the consciousness of his own purity. But if Christ came again, he might condemn the serene philosopher for his very serenity. For the Pharisee, we repeat, was righteous, if purity of intentions, together with a firm readiness to fulfil everything which appears to him in the light of duty, be righteousness in a man.

We jeer and laugh at a man not because he
is ridiculous, but because *we* want to have a
laugh out of him.   In the same way we are
indignant, not because this or the other act
is revolting to us, but because we want to let
off our steam.   But it does not follow from
this that we ought always to be calm and
smooth.   Woe to him who would try to
realise the ideal of justice on earth.

We think with peculiar intensity during
the hard moments of our life—we write when
we have nothing else to do.   So that a writer
can only communicate something of importance in reproducing the past.   When we are
driven to think, we have unfortunately no
mind to write, which accounts for the fact
that books are never more than a feeble echo
of what a man has gone through.

Tchekhov has a story called *Misfortune*
which well illustrates the difficulty a man
finds in adapting himself to a new truth, if
this truth threaten the security of his
condition.   The Merchant Avdeyer does not
believe that he is condemned, that he has

been brought to trial, and tried, and found guilty, for his irregularities in a public bank. He still thinks the verdict is yet to come—he still waits. In the world of learning something like this is happening. The educated have become so accustomed to think themselves not guilty, perfectly in the right, that they do not admit for a moment even now that they are brought to court. When threatening voices reach them, calling them to give an account of themselves, they only suspiciously shrug their shoulders. "All this will pass away"—they think. Well, when at last they are convinced that misfortune has befallen them, they will probably begin to justify themselves, like Avdeyer, declaring that they cannot even read printed matter sufficiently well. As yet, they pass for respectable, wise, experienced, omniscient men.

71

If a man had come to Dostoevsky and said to him, "I am hopelessly unhappy," the great artist in human misery would probably, at the bottom of his soul, have laughed at the naïveté of the poor creature. May one confess such things of oneself? May one go to such lengths of complaint, and still expect consolation from his neighbour?

Hopelessness is the most solemn and supreme moment in life. Till that point we have been assisted—now we are left to ourselves. Previously we had to do with men and human laws—now with eternity, and with the complete absence of laws. Is it not obvious ?

72

Byelinsky, in his famous letter, accuses Gogol, among other things, that in his *Correspondence with Friends*, he, Gogol, succumbs to the fear of death, of devils, and of hell. I find the accusation just : Gogol definitely feared death, demons, and hell. The point is, whether it is not right to fear these things, and whether fearlessness would be a proof of the high development of a man's soul. Schopenhauer asserts that death inspired philosophy. All the best poetry, all the wonderful mythology of the ancients and of modern peoples have for their source the fear of death. Only modern science forbids men to fear, and insists on a tranquil attitude towards death. So we arrive at utilitarianism and the positivist philosophy. If you wish to be rid of both these creeds you must be allowed to think again of death, and without shame to fear hell and its devils. It may be there is really a certain justification for concealing fears of such kind : in the ability to conceal one's agitation at moments of great danger there is a true beauty. But to deaden human sensitiveness and to keep the human intelligence within the bounds of perception, such a task can have charms only for a petty creature. Happily, mankind has no means by which to perform on itself such monstrous castration. Persecuted Eros, it is true, has hidden himself from the eyes of his enemies, but he has never abjured himself ; and even the strictest mediæval monks could not completely tear out their hearts from their breasts. Similarly with the aspiration towards the infinite : science persecuted it and put a veto on it. But laboratory workers themselves, sooner or later, recover their senses, and thirstily long to get out of the enclosure of positive knowledge, with that same thirsty longing that tortured the monks who wanted to get out of the enclosure of monastery walls.

73

If fate—and they say there is such a law— punishes criminals, it has its penalty also for the lovers of good. The former it throttles, the latter it spits upon. The former end in bitter torment, the latter—in ignominy.

74

Philosophy has always loved to occupy the position of a servant. In the Middle Ages she was the *ancilla theologiæ*, nowadays she waits on science. At the same time she calls herself the science of sciences.

75

I wonder which more effectually makes a man rush forwards without looking back: the knowledge that behind him hovers the head of Medusa, with horrible snakes, ready to turn him into stone; or the certainty that in the rear lies the unchangeable order laid down by the law of causality and by modern science. Judging from what we see, judging from the degree of tension which human thought has reached to-day, it would seem that the head of Medusa is less terrible than the law of causality. In order to escape the latter, man will face anything. Rather than return to the bosom of scientific cause and effect, he embraces madness: not that fine frenzy of madness which spends itself in fiery speeches, but technical madness, for which one is stowed away in a lunatic asylum.

76

" To experience a feeling of joy or sorrow, of triumph or despair, *ennui* or happiness, and so on, without having sufficient cause for such feeling, is an unfailing sign of mental disease . . . ." One of the modern truths which is seeing its last days.

77

Count Tolstoy's German biographer regrets the constant misunderstanding and quarrels which took place between Tolstoy and Turgenev. He reminds us of Goethe and Schiller, and thinks that Russian literature would have gained a great deal if the two remarkable Russian writers had been more pacific, had remained on constantly friendly terms with one another, and bequeathed to posterity a couple of volumes of letters dealing with literary and philosophic subjects. It might have been very nice—but I refuse to imagine Tolstoy and Turgenev keeping up a long, peaceful correspondence, particularly on high subjects. Nearly every one of Turgenev's opinions drove Tolstoy to madness, or was capable of so driving him. Dostoevsky's dislike of Turgenev was even stronger than Tolstoy's; he wrote of him very spitefully and offensively, libelling him rather than drawing a caricature. Evidently Dostoevsky, like Tolstoy, detested the " European " in their *confrère*. But here he was mistaken, in spite of his psychological acuteness. To Dostoevsky, it was enough that Turgenev wore European clothes and tried to appear like a westerner. He himself did the opposite : he tried to get rid of every trace of Europeanism from himself, apparently without great success, since he failed to make clear to himself wherein lay the strength of Europe, and where her sting. Nevertheless, the late Mikhailovsky is not wrong in calling Dostoevsky a seeker of buried treasure. Surely, in the second half of his literary activity Dostoevsky no longer sought for the real fruits of life. There awoke in him the Russian, the elemental man, with a thirst for the miraculous. Compared with what he wanted, the fruits of European civilisation seemed to him trivial, flat, insipid. The agelong civilisation of his neighbours told him that there never had been a miracle, and never would be. But all his being, not yet broken-in by civilisation, craved for the stupendous unknown. Therefore, the apparently-satisfied progressivist enraged him. Tolstoy once said of Turgenev : " I hate his democratic backside." Dostoev-

sky might have repeated these words . . .
And now, for the gratification of the German
critic, please reconcile the Russian writers
and make them talk serenely on high-flown
matters! Dostoevsky was within a hair's-
breath of a quarrel with Tolstoy, with whom,
not long before death interrupted him, he
began a long controversy concerning " Anna
Karenina." Even Tolstoy seemed to him too
compliant, too accommodating.

78

We rarely make a display of that which
is dear to us, near and dear and necessary.
On the other hand, we readily exhibit that
which is of no importance to us—there is
nothing else to be done with it. A man
takes his mistress to the theatre and sticks
her in full view of everybody ; he prefers to
remain at home with the woman he loves, or
to go about with her quietly, unnoticed.
So with our " Virtues." Every time we
notice in ourselves some quality we do not
prize we haste to make a show of it, thinking
perhaps that someone would be glad of it.
If it wins us approval, we are pleased—so
there is some gain. To an actor, a writer, or
an orator, his own antics, without which he
can have no success with the public, are often

disgusting. And yet his knack of making such antics he considers a talent, a divine gift, and he would rather die than that it should be lost to the public. Talent, on the whole, is accounted a divine gift, only because it is always on show, because it serves the public in some way or other. All our judgments are permeated through and through with utilitarianism, and were we to attempt to purify them from this adulteration what would remain of modern philosophy ? That is why youngish, inexperienced writers usually believe in *harmonia præstabilitata*, even though they have never heard of Leibnitz. They persuade themselves that there is no breach between egoistic and idealistic aspirations ; that, for instance, thirst for fame and desire to serve mankind are one and the same thing. Such a persuasion is usually very tenacious of life, and lasts long in men of vigorous and courageous mind. It seems to me that Poushkin would not have lost it, even had he lived to a prolonged old age. It was also part of Turgenev's belief—if a man of his spiritual fibre could have any belief. Tolstoy now believed, and now disbelieved, according to the work he had in hand. When he had other people's ideas to destroy he doubted the identity of egoistic

88

and idealist aspirations; when he had his
own to defend, he believed in it. Which is a
line of conduct worthy of attention, and
supremely worthy of imitation; for human
truths are proper exclusively for ancillary
purposes . . .

79

Man is such a conservative creature that
any change, even a change for the better,
scares him, he prefers the bad old way to the
new good one.   A man who has been all
his life a confirmed materialist would not
consent to believe that the soul was immortal,
not if it were proved to him *more geometrico*,
and not if he were a constitutional coward,
fearing death like Shakespeare's Falstaff.
Then we must take human conceit into
account.   Men do not like to admit themselves wrong.   It is absurd, but it is so.
Men, trivial, wretched creatures, proved by
history and by every common event to be
bunglers, yet must needs consider themselves infallible, omniscient.   What for?
Why not admit their ignorance flatly and
frankly?   True, it is easier said than done.
But why should slavish intellect, in spite of
our desire to be straightforward, deck us out
with would-be truths, of which we cannot
divest ourselves even when we know their

flimsiness.   Socrates wanted to think that he knew nothing—but he could not bring it off. He most absorbedly believed in his own knowledge; nothing could be "truth," except his teaching; he accepted the decree of the oracle, and sincerely esteemed himself the wisest of men.   And so it will be, as long as philosophers feel it their duty to teach and to save their neighbours. If a man wants to help people, he is bound to become a liar. We should undertake doubt seriously, not in order to return at length to established beliefs, for that would be a vicious circle. Experience shows us that such a process, certainly in the development of ultimate questions, only leads from error to error; we should doubt *so that doubt becomes a continuous creative force, inspiring the very essence of our life.* For established knowledge argues in us a condition of imperfect receptivity.   The weak, flabby spirit cannot bear quick, ceaseless change.   It must look round, it must have time to gather its wits, and so it must undergo the same experience time after time.   It needs the support and the security of habit.   But the well-grown soul despises your crutches.   He is tired of crawling on his own cabbage patch, he tears himself away from his own

" native " soil, and takes himself off into the far distances, braving the infinitude of space. Surely everybody knows we are not to live in the world for ever. But cowardice prevents one straightforward admitting of it, we keep it close till there is an occasion to air it as a truism. Only when misfortune, disease, old age come upon us, then the dread fear of departure walks with us like our own skeleton. We cannot dismiss him. At length, involuntarily, we begin to examine our gruesome companion with curiosity. And then, strangely enough, we observe that he not only tortures us, but, keeping pace with us, he has begun to gnaw through all the threads that bind us to the old existence. At moments it seems as if, a few more threads gone, nothing, nothing will remain to hold us back, the eternal dream of crawling man will be fulfilled, we shall be released from the bonds, we shall betake ourselves in liberty to regions far from this damned vale of earth. . . .

80

Moralists are abused because they offer us " moral consolations." This is not quite fair. Moralists would joyfully substitute palpable blessings for their abstract gifts, *if they could*. When he was young, Tolstoy wanted to make men happy ; when he was old, and knew he could not make them happy, he began to preach renunciation, resignation, and so forth. And how angry he got when people wouldn't have his teaching ! But if, instead of foisting his doctrines off on us as the solution of the ultimate problems, and as optimism, he had only spoken of the impossibility of finding satisfactory answers, and have offered himself as a pessimist, he would probably have obtained a much more willing hearing. Now he is annoying, because, finding himself unable to relieve his neighbours, he turns to them and insists that they shall consider themselves relieved by him, nay, even made happy by him. To which many will not agree : for why should they voluntarily renounce their rights ? Since although, God knows, the right of quarrelling with one's fate, and cursing it, is not a very grand right, still, it *is* a right . . .

81

Ivanov, in Tchekhov's drama of that name, compares himself to an overstrained labourer. The labourer dies, so that all that remains to Ivanov is to die. But logic, as you know, recommends great caution in coming to conclusions by analogy.

Behold Tchekhov himself, who, as far as we can judge, had endured in his own soul all the tragedy, just as Ivanov had, did not die or think of dying, or even turn out a wasted man. He is doing something, he struggles, he seeks, his work seems important and considerable to us, just like other human works. Ivanov shot himself because the drama *must* end, while Tchekhov had not yet finished his own struggle. Our æsthetics demand that the drama must have a climax and a finale: though we have abandoned the Aristotelian unities. Given a little more time, however, dramatic writers will have got rid of this restriction also. They will frankly confess that they do not know how, or with what event to end their dramas. Stories have already learnt to dispense with an ending.

82

More of the same.—Ivanov says: "Now, where is my salvation? In what? If an intelligent, educated, healthy man for no discoverable reason sets up a Lazarus lament and starts to roll down an inclined plane, then he is rolling without resisting, and there is no salvation for him." One way out would be to accept the inclined plane and the

93

gathering impetus as normal. Even further, one might find in the rolling descent a proof of one's spiritual superiority to other men. Of course in such a case one should go apart from the rest, not court young girls or fraternise with those who are living the ordinary life, but be alone. "Love is nonsense, caresses maudlin, work is meaningless, and song and fiery speeches are banal, played-out," continued Ivanov. To young Sasha these words are horrible,—but Ivanov will be responsible for them. He is already responsible for them. That he is tottering is nothing: it is still full early for him to shoot himself. He will live whilst his creator, Tchekhov, lives. And we shall listen to the shaky, vacillating philosophy. We are so sick of symmetry and harmony and finality, sick as we are of bourgeois self-complacency.

83

It will be seen from the above that already in *Ivanov*, one of his early works, Tchekhov has assumed the rôle of *advocatus diaboli*. Wherever Ivanov appears he brings ruin and destruction. It is true, Tchekhov hesitates to take his side openly, and evidently does not know what to do

94

with his hero, so that in the end he shakes him off, so to speak, he washes his hands of him in the accepted fashion: Ivanov shoots himself in the sight of everybody, has not even time to go discreetly into a corner. The only justification of *Ivanov* is that caricature of honesty, Doctor Lvov. Lvov is not a living figure—that is obvious. But this is why he is remarkable. It is remarkable that Tchekhov should deem it necessary to resurrect the forgotten Starodoum, that utterer of truisms in Fon-Visin's comedy; and to resurrect him no longer that people may bow their heads before the incarnation of virtue, but so that they shall jeer at him. Look at Doctor Lvov! Is he not Starodoum alive again? He is honesty personified. From force of old habit, honesty sticks his chest out, and speaks in a loud voice, with imperious tone, and yet not one of this old loyal subjects gives a brass farthing for him. They don't even trouble to gibe at him, but spit on him and shove him through the door, as a disgusting and impudent toady. Poor honesty! What has he sunk to! Evidently virtues, like everything else, should not live too long on earth.

Tchekhov's " Uncle Vanya " is waiting

to throw himself on the neck of his friend
and rival, the doctor, throw himself on his
neck and sob there like a little child, But
he finds that the doctor himself has an
unquenchable thirst for consolation and
encouragement, whilst poor Sonia can bear
her maiden sorrows no longer. They all
go wandering round with big, lost eyes,
looking for someone to relieve them from
part of their woes, at least. And lo, everybody is in the same street as themselves.
All are over-heavy-laden, not one can carry
his own burden, let alone give a lift to
another's. The last consolation is taken
away. It is no use complaining : there is no
sympathetic response. On all faces the'
same expression of hopelessness and despair.
Each must bear his cross in silence. None
may weep nor utter pitiful cries—it would be
uncalled-for and indecent. When Uncle
Vanya, who has not realised at once the
extremity of his situation, begins to cry
out : " My life's a waste ! " nobody wants
to listen to him. " Waste, waste ! Everybody knows it's a waste ! Shut your
mouth, howling won't help you : neither
will pistol-shots solve anything. Everyone
of us might start your cry—but we don't,
neither do we shout:

—You think I'll weep;
No, I'll not weep: I have full cause of weeping,
But this heart shall break into a hundred
  thousand flaws,
Or ere I'll weep ; O Fool, I shall go mad."

Gradually there settles down a dreadful, eternal silence of the cemetery. All go mad, without words, they realise what is happening within them, and make up their minds for the last shift : to hide their grief for ever from men, and to speak in commonplace, trivial words which will be accepted as sensible, serious, and even lofty expressions. No longer will anyone cry : " Life is a waste," and intrude his feelings on his neighbours. Everybody knows that it is shameful for one's life to be a waste, and that this shame should be hidden from every eye. The last law on earth is— loneliness . . . .

Résigne-toi, mon cœur, dors ton sommeil de brute !

85

Groundless assumptions. — " Based on nothing," because they seem to derive from common assumption of the reasonableness of human existence, which assumption surely is the child of our desires, and probably a

G

bastard at that . . . . . In his *Miserly Knight* Poushkin represented a miser as a romantic figure. Gogol, with his Plyushkin, creates on the contrary a repulsive figure of a miser. Gogol was nearer to reality. A miser is ugly, whatever view you take of him—inward or outward. Yet Gogol ought not to teach people to preserve in their age the ideals of their youth. Once old age is upon us—it must not be improved upon, much less apologised for. It must be accepted, and its essence brought to light. Plyushkin, the vulgar, dirty maniac is disgusting—but who knows ? perhaps he is fulfilling the serious mission of his own being. He is possessed by one desire—to everything else, to all happenings in the outer world he is indifferent. It is the same to him whether he is hungry or full, warm or cold, clean or dirty. Practically no event can distract his attention from his single purpose. He is disinterestedly mean, if one may say so. He has no need for his riches. He lets them rot in a disgusting heap, and does not dream, like Poushkin's knight, of palaces and power, or of sportive nymphs. Upon what end is he concentrated ? No one has the time to think it out. At the sight of Plyushkin everyone recalls the damage the miser has done. Everyone of course is right : Plyushkins, who heap up fortunes to let them rot, are very harmful. The social judgment is nearly always to the point. But not quite always. It won't hurt morals and social considerations if at times they have to hold their tongue—and at such times we might succeed in guessing the riddle of meanness, sordidness, old age.

86

We have sufficient grounds for taking life mistrustfully : it has defrauded us so often of our cherished expectations. But we have still stronger grounds for mistrusting reason : since if life deceived us, it was only because futile reason let herself be deceived. Perhaps reason herself invented the deception, and then to serve her own ambitious ends, threw the blame on life, so that life shall appear sick-headed. But if we have to choose between life and reason, we choose life, and then we no longer need try to foresee and to explain, we can wait, and accept all that is unalterable as part of the game. And thus Nietzsche, having realised that all his hopes had gradually crumbled, and that he could never get back to his former strength, but must grow worse and worse every day, wrote in a private letter of May 28, 1883: "*Ich will es so schwer haben, wie nur irgend ein Mensch es hat; erst unter diesem Drucke gewinne ich das gute Gewissen dafür, etwas zu besitzen, das wenige Menschen haben und gehabt haben: Flügel, um im Gleichnisse zu reden.*" In these few simple words lies the key to the philosophy of Nietzsche.

87

"So long as Apollo calls him not to the sacred offering, of all the trifling children of men the most trifling perhaps is the poet." Put Poushkin's expression into plain language, and you will get a page on neuropathology. All neurasthenic individuals sink from a state of extreme excitation to one of complete prostration. Poets too: and they are proud of it.

88

Shy people usually receive their impressions post-dated. During those moments when an event is taking place before their eyes, they can see nothing, only later on, having evoked from their memory a fragment of what happened, they make for themselves an impression of the whole scene.

And then, retrospectively arise in their soul feelings of pity, offence, surprise, so vivid, as if they were the flames of the instant moment, not rekindlings from the past. Thus shy people always think a great deal, and are always too late for their work. It is never too late for thought. Timid before others, they reach great heights of daring when alone. They are bad speakers—but often excellent writers. Their life is insignificant and tedious, they are not noticed,— until they become famous. And by the time fame comes, they do not need popular attention any more.

89

If Tchekhov's Layevsky, in *The Duel*, had been a writer with a literary talent, people would have said of him that he was original, and that he was engaged in the study of the "mysticism of sex," like Gabriele D'Annunzio for example; whereas, as he stands, he is only banal. His idleness is a reproach to him : people would prefer that at least he should copy out extracts from documents.

From observations on children.—Egoism in a man strikes us unpleasantly because it betrays our poverty. "I cannot dole out my abundance to my neighbour, for if I do I myself shall be left with little." We should like to be able to scatter riches with a royal hand; and, therefore, when we see someone else clutching his rags with the phrase, "property is sacred," we are hurt. What is sacred comes from the gods, and the gods have plenty of everything, they do not count and skimp, like mortals.

We see a man repent for his actions, and conclude that such actions should be avoided : an instance of false, but apparently irreproachable reasoning. Time passes, and we see the same man repenting again of the self-same acts. If we love logic, this will confirm us in our first conclusion. But if we do not care for logic, we shall say : man is under an equal necessity to commit these acts, and to repent of them. Sometimes, however, the first conclusion is corrected differently. Having decided that repentance proves that a certain course of action should be avoided, man avoids it all his life; only to realise in the end, suddenly, with extraordinary clarity, how bitter is his regret that he has not trodden the forbidden course. But by this time a new conclusion is already useless. Life is over, and the newly-enlightened mind no longer knows how to rid itself of the superfluous light.

92

A version of one of the scenes of Tolstoy's *Power of Darkness* reminds us exactly of a one-act piece of Maeterlinck. There can be no question of imitation. When the *Power of Darkness* was written nobody had heard of Maeterlinck. Tolstoy evidently wanted to try a new method of creating, and to get rid of his own manner, which he had evolved through tens of years of dogged labour. But the risk was too great. He preferred to cure himself of his doubts by the common expedient, manual toil and an outdoor life. So he took up the plough.

93

Every woodcock praises its own fen; Lermontov saw the sign of spiritual pre-eminence in dazzling white linen, and therefore his heroes always dressed with taste. Dostoevsky, on the other hand, despised

show: Dmitri Karamazov wears dirty
linen—and this is assigned to him as a merit,
or almost a merit.

94
While he was yet young, when he wrote
his story, *Enough*, Turgenev saw that something terrible hung over his life. He saw,
but did not get frightened, although he
understood that in time he ought to become
frightened, because life without a continual
inner disturbance would have no meaning
for him.

95
Napoleon is reputed to have had a
profound insight into the human soul;
Shakespeare also. And their vision has
nothing in common.

96
What we call imagination, which we
value so highly in great poets—is, essentially,
unbridled, loose, or if you will, even per-
verted mentality. In ordinary mortals we
call it vice; but to the poets everything is
forgiven on account of the benefit and
pleasure we derive from their works. In
spite of our high-flown theories we have
always been extremely practical, great

utilitarians. Two-and-a-half-thousand years went by before Tolstoy got up, and, in his turn, offered the poets their choice : either to be virtuous, or to stop creating and forfeit the fame of teachers. If Tolstoy did not make a laughing-stock of himself, he has to thank his grey hairs and the respect which was felt for his past. Anyhow, nobody took him seriously. Far from it; for never yet did poets feel so free from the shackles of morality as they do now. If Schiller were writing his dramas and philosophic essays to-day, he would scarcely find a reader. In Tolstoy himself it is not so much his virtues as his vices which we find interesting. We begin to understand his works, not so much in the light of his striving after ideals, but from the standpoint of that incongruity which existed between the ideas he artificially imposed upon himself, and the demands of his own non-virtuous soul, which struggled ever for liberty. Nicolenka Irtenyev, in *Childhood and Youth*, would sit for hours on the terrace, turning over in his mind his elder brother Volodya's love-making with the chambermaids. But, although he desired it "*more than anything on earth*," he could never bring himself to be like Volodya. The maid said to the elder brother, "Why doesn't Nicolai Petrovitch ever come here and have a lark?" She did not know that Nicolai Petrovitch was sitting at that moment under the stairs, ready to give *anything on earth* to take the place of the scamp Volodya. "*Everything on earth*" is twice repeated. Tolstoy gives a psychological explanation of his little hero's conduct. "I was timid by nature," Nicolenka tells us, "but my shyness was increased by the conviction of my ugliness." Ugliness, the consciousness of one's ugliness, leads to shyness! What good can there be in virtue which has such a suspicious origin? And how can the morality of Tolstoy's heroes be trusted? Consciousness of one's ugliness begets shyness, shyness drives the passions inwards and allows them no natural outlet. Little by little there develops a monstrous discrepancy between the imagination and its desires, on the one hand, and the power to satisfy these desires, on the other. Permanent hunger, and a contracted alimentary canal, which does not pass the food through. Hence the hatred of the imagination, with its unrealised and unrealisable cravings. . . . In our day no one has scourged love so cruelly as Tolstoy in *Power of Darkness*.

But the feats of the village Don Juan need not necessarily end in tragedy. "More than anything on earth," however, Tolstoy hates the Don Juans, the handsome, brave, successful, the self-confident, who spontaneously act upon suggestion, the conquerors of women, who stretch out their hands to living statues cold as stone. As far as ever he can he has his revenge on them in his writing.

97

In the drama of the future the whole presentation will be different. First of all, the difficulties of the dénouement will be set aside. The new hero has a past—reminiscent—but no present; neither wife, nor sweetheart, nor friends, nor occupation. He is alone, he communes only with himself or with imaginary listeners. He lives a life apart. So that the stage will represent either a desert island or a room in a large densely-populated city, where among millions of inhabitants one can live alone as on a desert island. The hero must not return to people and to social ideals. He must go forward to loneliness, to absolute loneliness. Even now nobody, looking at Gogol's Plyushkin, will feel any more the slightest response to the pathetic appeal for men to preserve the ideals of youth on into old age. Modern youths go to see Plyushkin, not for the sake of laughing at him or of benefiting from the warning which his terrible miserly figure offers them, but in order to see if there may not be some few little pearls there where they could be least expected, in the midst of his heap of dirt. . . . Lycurgus succeeded in fixing the Spartans like cement for some centuries —but after that came the thaw, and all their hardness melted. The last remains of the petrified Doric art are now removed to museums. . . . Is something happening—— ?

98

If I sow not in the spring, in autumn I shall eat no bread. Every day brings troubles and worries enough for poor, weak man. He had to forget his work for a moment, and now he is lost: he will die of hunger or cold. In order merely to preserve our existence we have to strain mind and body to the utmost: nay more, we have to think of the surrounding world exclusively with a view to gaining a livelihood from it. There is no time to think about truth! This is why positivism was invented, with its theory of natural development. Really, everything we see is mysterious and incomprehensible. A tiny midge and a huge elephant, a caressing breeze and a blizzard, a young tree and a rocky mountain—what are all these ? What are they, why are they ? we incessantly ask ourselves, but we may not speak out. For philosophy is ever pushed aside to make room for the daily needs. Only those think who are unable to trouble about self-preservation, or who will not trouble, or who are too careless : that is, sick, desperate, or lazy people. These return to the riddle which workaday men, confirmed in the certainty that they are right, have construed into " naturalness."

99

Kant, and after him Schopenhauer, was exceedingly fond of the epithet " disinterested," and used it on every occasion when the supply of laudatory terms he had at his disposal was exhausted. " Disinterested thinking," which does not pursue any practical aim, is, according to Schopenhauer, the highest ideal towards which man can strive. This truth he considered universal, an *a priori*. But had he chanced to be brought amongst Russian peasants he would have had to change his opinion. With them thoughts about destiny and the why and wherefore of the universe and infinity and so on, would by no means be considered disinterested, particularly if the man who devoted himself to such thoughts were at the same time to announce, as becomes a philosopher, that he claimed complete freedom from physical labour. There the philosopher, were he even Plato, would be stigmatised with the disgraceful nickname, "Idle-jack." There the highest activity is interested activity, directed towards strictly practical purposes; and if the peasants could speak learnedly, they would certainly call the principle upon which their judgment is founded an *a priori*. Tolstoy, who draws his wisdom from the folk-sources, attacks the learned for the very fact that they do not want to work, but are disinterestedly occupied in the search for truth.

100

It is clear to any impartial observer that practically every man changes his opinion ten times a day. Much has been said on this subject, it has served for innumerable satires and humorous sketches. Nobody has ever doubted that it was a vice to be unstable is one's opinions. Three-fourths of our education goes to teaching us most carefully to conceal within ourselves the changeableness of our moods and judgments. A man who cannot keep his word is the last of men: never to be trusted. Likewise, a man with no firm convictions: it is impossible to work together with him. Morality, here as always making towards utilitarian ends, issues the "eternal" principle: thou shalt remain true to thy convictions. In cultured circles this commandment is considered so unimpeachable that men are terrified even to appear inconstant in their own eyes. They become petrified in their beliefs, and no greater shame can happen to them than that they should be forced to admit that they have altered in their convictions. When a straightforward man like Montaigne plainly speaks of the inconstancy of his mind and his views, he is regarded as a libeller of himself. One need neither see, nor hear, nor understand what is taking place around one: once your mind is made up, you have lost your right to grow, you must remain a stock, a statue, the qualities and defects of which are known to everybody.

Every philosophic world-conception starts
from some or other solution of the general
problem of human existence, and proceeds
from this to direct the course of human
life in some particular direction or other.
We have neither the power nor the data
for the solution of general problems, and
consequently all our moral deductions are
arbitrary, they only witness to our prejudices
if we are naturally timid, or to our propensities and tastes if we are self-confident.
But to keep up prejudices is a miserable,
unworthy business : nobody will dispute
that. Therefore let us cease to grieve about
our differences in opinion, let us wish that
in the future there should be many more
differences, and much less unanimity. There
is no arbitrary truth : it remains to suppose
that truth lies in changeable human tastes
and desires. In so far as our common
social existence demands it—let us try
to come to an understanding, to agree :
but not one jot more. Any agreement
which does not arise out of common necessity
will be a crime against the Holy Spirit.

Tchekhov was very good at expounding a system of philosophy—even several systems. We have examples in more than one of his stories, particularly in *The Duel*, where Fon-Koren speaks *ex cathedra*. But Tchekhov had no use for such systems, save for purely literary purposes. When you write a story, and your hero must speak clearly and consistently, a system has its value. But when you are left to yourself, can you seriously trouble your soul about philosophy ? Even a German cannot, it seems, go so far in his " idealism." Vladimir Semionovitch, the young author in Tchekhov's *Nice People*, sincerely and deeply believes in his own ideas, but even of him, notwithstanding his blatantly comical limitations, we cannot say more than that his ideas were constant little views or pictures to him, which had gradually become a second natural setting to everything he saw. Certainly he did not live by ideas. Tchekhov is right when he says that the singing of *Gaudeamus igitur* and the writing of a humanitarian appeal were equally important to Vladimir Semionovitch. As soon as Vladimir's sister begins to think for herself, her brother's highest ideas,

which she has formerly revered, become
banal and objectionable to her. Her brother
cannot understand her, neither her hostility
to progress and humanitarianism, nor to
the university spree and *Gaudeamus igitur*.
But Tchekhov *does* understand. Only, let
us admit, the word "understand" does
not carry its ordinary meaning here. So
long as the child was fed on its mother's
milk, everything seemed to it smooth and
easy. But when it had to give up milk
and take to vodka,—and this is the
inevitable law of human development—
the childish suckling dreams receded into
the realm of the irretrievable past.

103

The summit of human existence, say
the philosophers, is spiritual serenity,
aequanimitas. But in that case the animals
should be our ideal, for in the matter of
imperturbability they leave nothing to be
desired. Look at a grazing sheep, or a
cow. They do not look before and after,
and sigh for what is not. Given a good
pasture, the present suffices them perfectly.

104

A hungry man was given a piece of bread, and a kind word. The kindness seemed more to him than the bread. But had he been given only the kind word and no bread, he would perhaps have hated nice phrases. Therefore, caution is always to be recommended in the drawing of conclusions: and in none more than in the conclusion that truth is more urgently required than a consoling lie. The connections of isolated phenomena can very rarely be discerned. As a rule, several causes at once produce one effect. Owing to our propensity for idealising, we always make prominent that cause which seems to us loftiest.

105

A strange anomaly! we see thousands of human beings perish around us, yet we walk warily lest we crush a worm. The sense of compassion is strong in us, but it is adapted to the conditions of our existence. It can relieve an odd case here and there— and it raises a terrific outcry over a trifling injustice. Yet Schopenhauer wanted to make compassion the metaphysical basis of morality.

106

To discard logic as an instrument, a means or aid for acquiring knowledge, would be extravagant. Why should we ? For the sake of consequentialism ? *i.e.* for logic's very self ? But logic, as an aim in itself, or even as the *only* means to knowledge, is a different matter. Against this one must fight even if he has against him all the authorities of thought—beginning with Aristotle.

107

" When the yellowing corn-fields sway and are moved, and the fresh forest utters sound to the breeze . . . then I see happiness on earth, and God in heaven." It may be so, to the poet ; but it may be quite different. Sometimes the corn-field waves, the woods make noise in the wind, the stream whispers its best tales : and still man cannot perceive happiness, nor forget the lesson taught in childhood, that the blue heavens are only an optical illusion. But if the sky and the boundless fields do not convince, is it possible that the arguments of Kant and the commentations of his dozens of talentless followers can do anything ?

108

The greatest temptation.—In Dostoevsky's *Grand Inquisitor* lurks a dreadful idea. Who can be sure, he says—metaphorically, of course—that when the crucified Christ uttered His cry: "Lord, why hast thou forsaken me?" He did not call to mind the temptation of Satan, who for one word had offered Him dominion over the world? And, if Jesus recollected this offer, how can we be sure that He did not repent not having taken it? . . . One had better not be told about such temptations.

109

From the *Future Opinions concerning contemporary Europe."*—" Europe of the nineteenth and twentieth centuries presented a strange picture. After Luther, Christianity degenerated into morality, and all the threads connecting man with God were cut. Together with the rationalisation of religion, all life took on a flat, rational character. Knights were replaced by a standing army, recruited on the principle of compulsory military service for all, and existing chiefly for the purpose of parades and official needs. Alchemy, which had been trying to find the philosopher's stone, was replaced by chemistry, which tried to discover the best means for cheap preparation of cheap commodities. Astrology, which had sought in the stars the destinies of men, was replaced by astronomy, which foretold the eclipses of the sun and the appearing of comets. Even the dress of the people became strangely colourless; not only men, but women also wore uniform, monochromatic clothes. Most remarkable of all, that epoch did not notice its own insignificance, but was even proud of itself. It seemed to the man of that day that never before had the common treasury of spiritual riches been so well replenished. We, of course, may smile at their naïveté, but if one of their own number had allowed himself to express an opinion disdainful of the bases of the contemporary culture he would have been declared immoral, or put away in a mad-house: a terrible punishment, very common in that coarse period, though now it is very difficult even to imagine what such a proceeding implied. But in those days, to be known as immoral, or to find oneself in a mad-house, was worse than to die. One of the famous poets of the nineteenth century, Alexander Poushkin, said: 'God forbid that I should go mad. Rather let me be a starving beggar.' In those times people, on the whole, were compelled to tell lies and play the hypocrite, so that not infrequently the brightest minds, who saw through the shams of their epoch, yet pretended to believe in science and morality, only in order to escape the persecution of public opinion."

110

Writers of tragedies on Shakespeare's model. —To obtain a spark, one must strike with all one's might with an iron upon a stone. Whereupon there is a loud noise, which many are inclined to believe more important than the little spark. Similarly, writers having shouted very loudly, are deeply assured that they have fulfilled their sacred mission, and are amazed that all do not share their raptures, that some even stop their ears and run away.

111

Metamorphoses.—Sense and folly are not at all native qualities in a man. In a crisis, a stupid man becomes clever. We need not go far for an example. What a gaping simpleton Dostoevsky looks in his *Injured and Insulted,* not to mention *Poor Folk.* But in *Letters from the Underworld*

and the rest of his books he is the shrewd-
est and cleverest of writers. The same
may be said of Nietzsche, Tolstoy, or
Shakespeare. In his *Birth of Tragedy*
Nietzsche seems just like the ordinary honest,
rather simple, blue-eyed provincial German
student, and in *Zarathustra* he reminds
one of Machiavelli. Poor Shakespeare got
himself into a row for his Brutus—but no
man could deny the great mind in *Hamlet*.
The best instance of all, however, is Tolstoy.
Right up to to-day, whenever he likes he
can be cleverer than the cleverest. Yet at
times he is a schoolboy. This is the most
interesting and enviable trait in him.

112

In *Troilus and Cressida* Thersites says :
" Shall the elephant Ajax carry it thus ?
He beats me, and I rail at him : O worthy
satisfaction ! would it were otherwise ; that
I could beat him, whilst he railed at me."
Dostoevsky might have said the same of
his opponents. He pursued them with
stings, sarcasm, abuse, and they drove
him to a white heat by their quiet assurance
and composure. . . . The present-day admirers of Dostoevsky *quietly believe* in the
teachings of their master. Does it not

120

mean that *de facto* they have betrayed him
and gone over to the side of his enemies.

The opinion has gained ground that
Turgenev's ideal women—Natalie, Elena,
Marianna—are created in the image and
likeness of Poushkin's Tatyana. The critics
have been misled by external appearances.
To Poushkin his Tatyana appears as a
vestal guarding the sacred flame of high
morality—because such a job is not fitting
for a male. The Pretender in *Boris Godunov*
says to the old monk Pimen, who preaches
meekness and submission : " But you fought
under the walls of Kazan, etc." That is
a man's work. But in the hours of peace
and leisure the fighter needs his own hearth-
side, he must feel assured that at home his
rights are safely guarded. This is the point
of Tatyana's last words : " I belong to
another, and shall remain forever true to
him." But in Turgenev woman appears
as the judge and the reward, sometimes
even the inspirer of victorious man. There
is a great difference.

From a German *Introduction to Philosophy*.
—" We shall maintain the opinion that metaphysics, as the crown of the particular
sciences, is possible and desirable, and that
to it falls the task intermediate between
theory and practice, experiment and anticipa-
tion, mind and feeling, the task of weighing
probabilities, balancing arguments, and
reconciling difficulties." Thus metaphysics
is a weighing of probabilities. *Ergo*—further
than probable conclusions it cannot go.
Thus why do metaphysicians pretend to
universal and obligatory, established and
eternal judgments ? They go beyond themselves. In the domain of metaphysics there
cannot and must not be any established
beliefs. The word established loses all its
sense in the connection. It is reasonable
to speak of eternal hesitation and temporality
of thought.

From another *Introduction to Philosophy*,
also German. " Compared with the delusion
of the materialists . . . the wretchedest
worshipper of idols seems to us a being
capable of apprehending to a certain degree
the great meaning and essence of things."
Perhaps this thought strayed in accidentally

among the huge herd of the other thoughts
of the professor, so little does it resemble the
rest. But even so, it loses none of its interest.
If the materialists here spoken of, those of the
nineteenth century, Büchner, Vogt, Moleschot, all of them men who stood on the
pinnacle of natural science, were capable of
proving in the realm of philosophy more
uninformed than the nakedest savage, then
it follows, not only that science has nothing
in common with philosophy, but that the
two are even hostile. Therefore we ought
to go to the savages, not to civilise them,
but even to learn philosophy from them. A
Papuan or a Tierra del Fuegan delivering
a lecture in philosophy to the professors
of the Berlin University—Friedrich Paulsen,
for example—is a curious sight. I say to
Friedrich Paulsen, and not to Büchner or
Moleschot, because Paulsen is also an
educated person, and therefore his *philosophic*
sensibility may have suffered from contact
with science, even if not so badly as that
of the materialists. He needs the assistance
of a red-skinned master. Why have German
professors so little daring or enterprise ?
Why should not Paulsen, on his own in-
itiative, go to Patagonia to perfect himself
in philosophy ?—or at least send his pupils

there, and preach broadcast the new pilgrimage. And now lo and behold he has hatched an original and fertile idea, so he will stick in a corner with it, so that even if you wanted you could not get a good look at it. The idea is important and weighty : our philosophers would lose nothing by sitting at the feet of the savages.

116

From a *History of Ethics.*—" Doubts concerning the existence or the possibility of discovering a moral norm have, *of course* (I underline it), proved a stimulus to a new speculative establishing of ethics, just as the denial of the possibility of knowledge led to the discovery of the condition of knowledge." With this proposition the author does not play hide-and-seek, as Paulsen with his. He places it in a conspicuous position, in a conspicuous section of his book, and accompanies it with the trumpeting herald " of course." But only one thing is clear : namely, that the majority share the opinion of Professor Yodl, to whom the quoted words belong. So that the first assumption of ethics has as its foundation the *consensus sapientium.* It is enough.

" The normative theory," which has taken such hold in Germany and Russia, bears the stamp of that free and easy self-assurance which characterises the state of contentment, and which does not desire, even for the sake of theoretical perfection, to take into consideration the divided state of soul which usually accompanies discontent. Windelband (*Praeludien*, p. 313) is evidence of this. He exposes himself with the naïve frankness almost of an irrational creature, and is not only unashamed, but even proud of his part. " Philosophic research," he says, " is possible only to those who are convinced that the norm of the universal imperative is supreme above individual activities, and that such a norm is discoverable." Not every witness will give evidence so honestly. It amounts to this : that philosophic research is not a search after truth, but a conspiracy amongst people who *dethrone truth* and exalt instead the all-binding norm. The task is truly ethical : morality always was and always will be utilitarian and bullying. Its active principle is : He who is not with us, is against us.

"If, besides the reality which is evident to us, we were susceptible to another form of reality, chaotic, lawless, then this latter could not be the subject of thought." (Riehl—*Philosophie der Gegenwart.*) This is one of the *a priori* of critical philosophy—one of the unproved first assumptions, evidently. It is only an expression in other words of Windelband's assertion quoted above, concerning the ethical basis of the law of causation. Thus, the *a priori* of contemporary thought convince us more and more that Nietzsche's instinct was not at fault. The root of all our philosophies lies, not in our objective observations, but in the demands of our own heart, in the subjective, moral *will*, and therefore science cannot be uprooted except we first destroy morality.

One of the lofty truisms—"The philosopher conquers passion by perceiving it, the artist by bodying it forth." In German it sounds still more lofty : but does not for that reason approach any nearer to the truth. "*Der Philosoph überwindet die Leidenschaft, indem er sie begreift—der*

Künstler, indem er sie darstellt." (Windelband, *Praeludien*, p. 198.)

120

The Germans always try to get at
Allgemeingültigkeit. Well, if the problem
of knowledge is to fathom all the depths
of actual life, then experience, in so far as
it repeats itself, is uninteresting, or at least
has a limit of interest. It is necessary,
however, to know what nobody yet knows,
and therefore we must walk, not on the
common road of *Allgemeingültigkeit,* but on
new tracks, which have never yet seen
human feet. Thus morality, which lays
down definite rules and thereby guards life
for a time from any surprise, exists only by
convention, and in the end collapses before
the non-moral surging-up of individual
human aspirations. Laws—all of them—
have only a regulating value, and are necessary only to those who want rest and
security. But the first and essential condition of life is lawlessness. Laws are a
refreshing sleep—lawlessness is creative
activity.

A = A.—They say that logic does not need this postulate, and could easily develop it by deduction. I think not. On the contrary, in my opinion, logic could not exist without this premiss. Meanwhile it has a purely empirical origin. In the realm of fact, A is always more or less equal to A. But it might be otherwise. The universe might be so constituted as to admit of the most fantastic metamorphoses. That which now equals A would successively equal B and then C, and so on. At present a stone remains long enough a stone, a plant a plant, an animal an animal. But it might be that a stone changed into a plant before our eyes, and the plant into an animal. That *there is nothing unthinkable* in such a supposition is proved by the theory of evolution. This theory only puts centuries in place of seconds. So that, in spite of the risk to which I expose myself from the admirers of the famous Epicurean system, I am compelled to repeat once more that anything you please may come from anything you please, that A may not equal A, and that consequently logic is dependent, for its soundness, on the empirically-derived law of the unchangeableness of the external

world. Admit the possibility of super-
natural interference—and logic will lose that
certitude and inevitability of its conclusions
which at present is so attractive to us.

122

The effort to *understand* people, life, the
universe prevents us from getting to know
them at all. Since "to know" and "to
understand" are two concepts which are
not only non-identical, but just the opposite
of one another in meaning ; in spite of their
being in constant use as synonyms. We
think we have understood a phenomenon
if we have included it in a list of others,
previously known to us. And, since all our
mental aspiration reduces itself to understanding the universe, we refuse to know a
great deal which will not adapt itself to the
plane surface of the contemporary world-
conceptions. For instance the Leibnitz
question, put by Kant into the basis of the
critique of reason : "How can we know a
thing outside us, if it does not enter into
us ?" It is non-understandable ; that is,
it does not agree with our notion of understanding. Hence it follows that it must be
squeezed out of the field of view—which is
exactly what Kant attempted to do. To

us it seems, on the contrary, that in the interests of *knowing* we should sacrifice, and gladly, understanding, since understanding in any case is a secondary affair.— *Zu fragmentarish ist Welt und Leben!* . . .

PART II

Nur für Schwindelfreie.

(From *Alpine Recollections.*)

I

LIGHT reveals to us beauty—but also ugliness. Throw vitriol in the face of a beautiful woman, and the beauty is gone, no power on earth will enable us to look upon her with the same rapture as before. Could even the sincerest, deepest love endure the change? True, the idealists will hasten to say that love overcomes all things. But idealism needs be prompt, for if she leaves us one single moment in which to *see*, we shall see such things as are not easily explained away. That is why idealists stick so tight so logic. In the twinkling of an eye logic will convey us to the remotest conclusions and forecasts. Reality could never overtake her. Love is eternal, and consequently a disfigured face will seem as lovely to us as a fresh one. This is, of course, a lie, but it helps to preserve old tastes and obscures danger. Real danger, however, was never dispelled by words. In spite of Schiller and eternal love, in the long run vitriol triumphs, and the agreeable young man is forced to abandon his beloved and acknowledge himself a fraud. Light, the source of his life and hope, has now destroyed hope and life for him. He will not return to idealism, and he will hate logic: light, that seemed to him so beautiful, will have become hideous. He will turn to darkness, where logic and its binding conclusions have no power, but where the fancy is free for all her vagaries. Without light we should never have known that vitriol ruins beauty. No science, nor any art can give us what darkness gives. It is true, in our young days when all was new, light brought us great happiness and joy. Let us, therefore, remember it with gratitude, as a benefactor we no longer need. Do after all let us dispense with gratitude, for it belongs to the calculating, bourgeois virtues. *Do ut des.* Let us forget light, and gratitude, and the qualms of self-important idealism, let us go bravely to meet the coming night. She promises us great power over reality. Is it worth while to give up our old tastes and lofty convictions? Love and light have not availed against vitriol. What a horror would have seized us at the thought, once upon a time! That short phrase

can annul all Schiller. We have shut our
eyes and stopped our ears, we have built
huge philosophic systems to shield us from
this tiny thought. And now—now it seems
we have no more feeling for Schiller and
the great systems, we have no pity on our
past beliefs. We now are seeking for words
with which to sing the praises of our former
enemy. Night, the dark, deaf, impenetrable
night, peopled with horrors—does she not
now loom before us, infinitely beautiful?
Does she not draw us with her still, mysterious, fathomless beauty, far more powerfully
than noisy, narrow day? It seems as if,
in a short while, man will feel that the same
incomprehensible, cherishing power which
threw us out into the universe and set us,
like plants, to reach to the light, is now
gradually transferring us to a new direction,
where a new life awaits us with all its stores.
Fata volentem ducunt, nolentem trahunt.
And perhaps the time is near when the
impassioned poet, casting a last look to his
past, will boldly and gladly cry:

Hide thyself, sun! O darkness, be welcome!

2

Psychology at last leads us to conclude
that the most generous human impulses
spring from a root of egoism. Tolstoy's
"love to one's neighbour," for example,
proves to be a branch of the old self-love.
The same may be said of Kant's idealism,
and even of Plato's. Though they glorify
the service of the idea, in practice they
succeed in getting out of the vicious circle
of egoism no better than the ordinary
mortal, who is neither a genius nor a flower
of culture. In my eyes this is "almost"
an absolute truth. (It is never wrong to
add the retractive "almost"; truth is too
much inclined to exaggerate its own importance, and one must guard oneself against its
despotic authority.) Thus—all men are
egoists. Hence follows a great deal. I
even think this proposition might provide
better grounds for metaphysical conclusions
than the doubtful capacity for compassion
and love for one's neighbour which has been
so tempting to dogma. For some reason
men have imagined that love for oneself
is more natural and comprehensible than
love for another. Why ? Love for others
is only a little rarer, less widely diffused
than love to oneself. But then hippopotami

and rhinoceros, even in their own tropical regions, are less frequent than horses and mules. Does it follow that they are less natural and transcendental? Positivism is not incumbent upon blood-thirsty savages. Nay, as we know, many of them are less positive-minded than our learned men. For instance, a future life is to them such an infallible reality that they even enter into contracts, part of which is to be fulfilled in the next world. A German metaphysician won't go as far as that. Hence it follows that the way to know the other world is not by any means through love, sympathy, and self-denial, as Schopenhauer taught. On the contrary, it appears as if love for others were only an impediment to metaphysical flights. Love and sympathy chain the eye to the misery of this earth, where such a wide field for active charity opens out. The materialists were mostly very good men—a fact which bothered the historians of philosophy. They preached Matter, believed in nothing, and were ready to perform all kinds of sacrifices for their neighbours. How is this? It is a case of clearest logical consequence: man loves his neighbour, he sees that heaven is indifferent to misery, therefore he takes upon himself the rôle of Providence. Were he indifferent to the sufferings of others, he would easily become an idealist and leave his neighbours to their fate. Love and compassion kill belief, and make a man a positivist and a materialist in his philosophical outlook. If he feels the misery of others, he leaves off meditating and wants to act. Man only thinks properly when he realises he has nothing to do, his hands are tied. That is why any profound thought must arise from despair. Optimism, on the other hand, the readiness to jump hastily from one conclusion to another, may be regarded as an inevitable sign of narrow self-sufficiency, which dreads doubt and is consequently always superficial. If a man offers you a solution of eternal questions, it shows he has not even begun to think about them. He has only " acted." Perhaps it is not necessary to think—who can say how we ought or ought not to live ? And how could we be brought to live " as we ought," when our own nature is and always will be an incalculable mystery. There is no mistake about it, nobody *wants* to think. I do not speak here of logical thinking. That, like any other natural function, gives man great pleasure. For this reason philosophical systems, however complicated, arouse real and permanent interest in the public provided they only require from man the logical exercise of the mind, and nothing else. But to think—really to think—surely this means a relinquishing of logic. It means living a new life. It means a permanent sacrifice of the dearest habits, tastes, attachments, without even the assurance that the sacrifice will bring any compensation. Artists and philosophers like to imagine the thinker with a stern face, a profound look which penetrates into the unseen, and a noble bearing—an eagle preparing for flight. Not at all. A thinking man is one who has lost his balance, in the vulgar, not in the tragic sense. Hands raking the air, feet flying, face scared and bewildered, he is a caricature of helplessness and pitiable perplexity. Look at the aged Turgenev, his Poems in Prose and his letter to Tolstoy. Maupassant thus tells of his meeting with Turgenev: "There entered a giant with a silvery head." Quite so! The majestic patriarch and master, of course! The myth of giants with silver locks is firmly established in the heart of man. Then suddenly enters Turgenev in his Prose Poems—pale, pitiful, fluttering like a bird that has been " winged." Turgenev, who has taught us everything—how can he be so fluttered and bewildered ? How could he write his letter to Tolstoy ? Did he not know that Tolstoy was finished, the source of his creative activity dried up, that he must seek other activities. Of course he knew—and still he wrote that letter. But it was not for Tolstoy, nor even for Russian literature, which, of course, is not kept going by the death-bed letters and covenants of its giants. In the dreadful moments of the end, Turgenev, in spite of his noble size and silver locks, did not know what to say or where to look for support and consolation. So he turned to literature, to which he had given his life. . . . He yearned that she, whom he had served so long and loyally, should just once help him, save him from the horrible and thrice senseless nightmare. He stretched out his withered, numbing hands to the printed sheets which still preserve the traces of the soul of a living, suffering man. He addressed his late enemy Tolstoy with the most flattering name : " Great writer of the Russian land " ; recollected that he was his contemporary, that he himself was a great writer of the Russian land. But this he

did not express aloud. He only said, "I
can no longer——" He praised a strict
school of literary and general education.
To the last he tried to preserve his bearing
of a giant with silvery locks. And we were
gratified. The same persons who are indignant at Gogol's correspondence, quote Turgenev's letter with reverence. The attitude
is everything. Turgenev knew how to pose
passably well, and this is ascribed to him as
his greatest merit. *Mundus vult decipi,
ergo decipiatur.* But Gogol and Turgenev
felt substantially the same. Had Turgenev
burnt his own manuscripts and talked of
himself instead of Tolstoy, before death,
he would have been accounted mad. Moralists would have reproached him for his
display of extreme egoism. . . . And Philosophy ? Philosophy seems to be getting rid
of certain prejudices. At the moment when
men are least likely to play the hypocrite
and lie to themselves Turgenev and Gogol
placed their personal fate higher than the
destinies of Russian literature. Does not
this betray a "secret" to us ? Ought we
not to see in absolute egoism an inalienable
and great, yes, very great quality of human
nature ? Psychology, ignoring the threats
of morality, has led us to a new knowledge.

141

Yet still, in spite of the instances we have given, the mass of people will, as usual, see nothing but malice in every attempt to reveal the human impulses that underlie "lofty" motives. To be merely men seems humiliating to men. So now malice will also be detected in my interpretation of Turgenev's letter, no matter what assurance I offer to the contrary.

3

On Method.—A certain naturalist made the following experiment: A glass jar was divided into two halves by a perfectly transparent glass partition. On the one side of the partition he placed a pike, on the other a number of small fishes such as form the prey of the pike. The pike did not notice the partition, and hurled itself on its prey, with, of course, the result only of a bruised nose. The same happened many times, and always the same result. At last, seeing all its efforts ended so painfully, the pike abandoned the hunt, so that in a few days, when the partition had been removed it continued to swim about among the small fry without daring to attack them. . . . Does not the same happen with us ? Perhaps the limits between " this

142

world" and "the other world" are also essentially of an experimental origin, neither rooted in the nature of things, as was thought before Kant, or in the nature of our reason, as was thought after Kant. Perhaps indeed a partition does exist, and make vain all attempts to cross over. But perhaps there comes a moment when the partition is removed. In our minds, however, the conviction is firmly rooted that it is impossible to pass certain limits, and painful to try: a conviction founded on experience. But in this case we should recall the old scepticism of Hume, which idealist philosophy has regarded as mere subtle mind-play, valueless after Kant's critique. The most lasting and varied experience cannot lead to any binding and universal conclusion. Nay, all our *a priori*, which are so useful for a certain time, become sooner or later extremely harmful. A philosopher should not be afraid of scepticism, but should go on bruising his jaw. Perhaps the failure of metaphysics lies in the caution and timidity of metaphysicians, who seem ostensibly so brave. They have sought for rest—which they describe as the highest boon. Whereas they should have valued more than anything restlessness, aimlessness, even

143

purposelessness. How can you tell when the partition will be removed? Perhaps at the very moment when man ceased his painful pursuit, settled all his questions and rested on his laurels, inert, he could with one strong push have swept through the pernicious fence which separated him from the unknowable. There is no need for man to move according to a carefully-considered plan. This is a purely æsthetic demand which need not bind us. Let man senselessly and deliriously knock his head against the wall—if the wall go down at last, will he value his triumph any the less? Unfortunately for us the illusion has been established in us that plan and purpose are the best guarantee of success. What a delusion it is! The opposite is true. The best of all that genius has revealed to us has been revealed as the result of fantastic, erratic, apparently ridiculous and useless, but relentlessly stubborn seeking. Columbus, tired of sitting on the same spot, sailed west to look for India. And genius, in spite of vulgar conception, is a condition of chaos and unutterable restlessness. Not for nothing has genius been counted kin to madness. Genius flings itself hither and thither because it has not the *Sitzfleisch*

necessary for industrious success in mediocrity. We may be sure that earth has
seen much more genius than history has
recorded; since genius is acknowledged
only when it has been serviceable. When
the tossing-about has led to no useful issue
—which is the case in the majority of
instances—it arouses only a feeling of
disgust and abomination in all witnesses.
" He can't rest and he can't let others rest."
If Lermontov and Dostoevsky had lived in
times when there was no demand for books,
nobody would have noticed them. Lermontov's early death would have passed
unregretted. Perhaps some settled and
virtuous citizen would have remarked, weary
of the young man's eternal and dangerous
freaks: "For a dog a dog's death." The
same of Gogol, Tolstoy, Poushkin. Now they
are praised because they left interesting
books. . . . And so we need pay no attention to the cry about the futility and worth-
lessness of scepticism, even scepticism pure
and unadulterated, scepticism which has
no ulterior motive of clearing the way for a
new creed. To knock one's head against
the wall out of hatred for the wall: to
beat against established and obstructive
ideas, because one detests them: is it not

an attractive proposition ? And then, to
see ahead uncertainly and limitless possibilities, instead of up-to-date "ideals," is
not this too fascinating ? The highest good
is rest ! I shall not argue : *de gustibus
aut nihil aut bene.* . . . By the way, isn't
it a superb principle ? And this superb
principle has been arrived at perfectly by
chance, unfortunately not by me, but by
one of the comical characters in Tchekhov's *Seagull.* He mixed up two Latin
proverbs, and the result was a splendid
maxim which, in order to become an *a
priori*, awaits only universal acceptance.

4

Metaphysicians praise the transcendental,
and carefully avoid it. Nietzsche hated
metaphysics, he praised the earth—*bleib
nur der Erde treu, O meine Bruder*—and
always lived in the realm of the transcendental. Of course the metaphysicians behave better : this is indisputable. He who
would be a teacher must proclaim the metaphysical point of view, and he may become
a hero without ever smelling powder. In
these anxious days, when positivism seems
to fall short, one cannot do better than turn
to metaphysics. Then the young man need

not any more envy Alexander the Mace-
donian. With the assistance of a few books
not only earthly states are conquered, but
the whole mysterious universe. Metaphysics
is the great art of swerving round dangerous
experience. So metaphysicians should be
called the positivists *par excellence*. They
do not despise all experience, as they assert,
but *only the dangerous experiences*. They
adapt the safest of all methods of self-
defence, what the English call protective
mimicry. Let us repeat to all students—
professors know it already : he who would
be a sincere metaphysician must avoid
risky experience. Schiller once asked : How
can tragedy give delight ? The answer
—to put it in our own words—was : If we
are to obtain delight from tragedy, it must
be seen only upon the stage.—In order to
love the transcendental it also should be
known only from the stage, or from books
of the philosophers. This is called idealism,
the nicest word ever invented by philoso-
phising men.

5

Poetae nascuntur.—Wonderful is man.
Knowing nothing about it, he asserts the
existence of an objective impossibility. Even
a little while ago, before the invention of

the telephone and telegraph, men would have declared it impossible for Europe to converse with America. Now it is possible. We cannot produce poets, therefore we say they are born. Certainly we cannot make a child a poet by forcing him to study literary models, from the most ancient to the most modern. Neither will anybody hear us in America no matter how loud we shout here. To make a poet of a man, he must not be developed along ordinary lines. Perhaps books should be kept from him. Perhaps it is necessary to perform some apparently dangerous operation on him : fracture his skull or throw him out of a fourth-storey window. I will refrain from recommending these methods as a substitute for paedagogy. But that is not the point. Look at the great men, and the poets. Except John Stuart Mill and a couple of other positivist thinkers, who had learned fathers and virtuous mothers, none of the great men can boast of, or better, complain of, a proper upbringing. In their lives nearly always the decisive part was played by accident, accident which reason would dub meaninglessness, if reason ever dared raise its voice against obvious success. Something like a broken

skull or a fall from the fourth floor—not
metaphorically, but often absolutely literally
—has proved the commencement, usually
concealed but occasionally avowed, of the
activity of genius. But we repeat automatically : *poetae nascuntur*, and are deeply
convinced that this extraordinary truth
is so lofty it needs no verification.

6

" Until Apollo calls him to the sacrifice,
ignobly the poet is plunged in the cares
of this shoddy world ; silent is his lyre,
cold sleeps his soul, of all the petty children
of earth most petty it seems is he." Pisaryev,
the critic, was exasperated by these verses.
Presumably, if they had not belonged to
Poushkin, all the critics along with Pisaryev
would have condemned them and their
author to oblivion. Suspicious verse !
Before Apollo calls to him—the poet is
the most insignificant of mortals ! In his
free hours, the ordinary man finds some
more or less distinguished distraction for
himself : he hunts, attends exhibitions of
pictures, or the theatre, and finally rests
in the bosom of his family. But the poet
is incapable of normal existence. Im-
mediately he has finished with Apollo,

forgetting all about altars and sacrifices, he proceeds to occupy himself with unworthy objects. Or he abandons himself to the *dolce far niente*, the customary pastime of all favourites of the Muses. Let us here remark that not only all poets, but all writers and artists in general are inclined to lead bad lives. Think what Tolstoy tells us, in *Confession* and elsewhere, of the best representatives of literature in the fifties. On the whole it is just as Poushkin says in his verses. Whilst he is engaged in composition, an author is a creature of some consequence : apart from this, he is nothing. Why are Apollo and the Muses so remiss? Why do they draw to themselves wayward or vicious votaries, instead of rewarding virtue? We dare not suspect the gods, even the de-throned, of bad intentions. Apollo loved virtuous persons—and yet virtuous persons are evidently mediocre and unfit for the sacred offices. If any man is overcome with a great desire to serve the god of song, let him get rid of his virtues at once. Curious that this truth is so completely unknown to men. They think that through virtue they can truly deserve the favour and choice of Apollo. And since industry is the first virtue, they peg away, morning, noon, and night. Of course, the more they work the less they do. Which really puzzles and annoys them. They even fling aside the sacred arts, and all the labours of a devotee; they give themselves up to idleness and other bad habits. And sometimes it so happens, that just as a man decides that it is all no good, the Muses suddenly visit him. So it was with Dostoevsky and others. Schiller alone managed to get round Apollo. But perhaps it was only his biographers he got round. Germans are so trustful, so easy to deceive. The biographers saw nothing unusual in Schiller's habit of keeping his feet in cold water whilst he worked. No doubt they felt that if the divine poet had lived in the Sahara, where water is precious as gold, and the inspired cannot take a footbath every day, then the speeches of the Marquis of Pola would have lacked half their nobleness, at least. And apparently Schiller was not so wonderfully chaste, if he needed such artificial resources in the composition of his fine speeches. In a word, we must believe Poushkin. A poet is, on the one hand, among the elect; on the other hand, he is one of the most insignificant of mortals.

Hence we can draw a very consoling conclusion : the most insignificant of men are not altogether so worthless as we imagine. They may not be fit to occupy government positions or professorial chairs, but they are often extremely at home on Parnassus and such high places. Apollo rewards vice, and virtue, as everybody knows, is so satisfied with herself she needs no reward. Then why do the pessimists lament? Leibnitz was quite right : we live in the best possible of worlds. I would even suggest that we leave out the modification "possible."

7

It is *Das Ewig Weibliche*, with Russian writers. Poushkin and Lermontov loved women and were not afraid of them. Poushkin, who trusted his own nature, was often in love, and always sang his love of the moment. When infatuated with a bacchante, he glorified bacchantes. When he married, he warbled of a modest, nunlike beauty, his wife. A synthesising mind would probably not know what to do with all Poushkin's sorts of love. Nor is Lermontov any better. He abused women, but, as Byelinsky observed after meeting him, he loved women more than anything in

the world. And again, not women of one
mould only : any and all attractive females :
the wild Bella, the lovely Mary, Thamar ;
one and all, no matter of what race or
condition. Every time Lermontov is in
love, he assures us his love is so deep and
ardent and even moral, that we cannot
judge him without conpunction. Vladimir
Soloviov alone was not afraid to condemn
him. He brought Poushkin as well as
Lermontov to account for their moral
irregularities, and he even went so far as
to say that it was not he himself who judged
them, but Fate, in whose service he acted
as public denouncer. Lermontov and Poushkin, both dying young, had deserved death
for their frivolities. But there was nobody
else besides Vladimir Soloviov to darken the
memories of the two poets. It is true Tolstoy
cannot forgive Poushkin's dissolute life,
but he does not apply to Fate for a verdict.
According to Tolstoy morality can cope
even with a Titan like Poushkin. In Tolstoy's
view morality grows stronger the harder
the job it has to tackle. It pardons the
weak offenders without waste of words,
but it never forgives pride and self-confi-
dence. If Tolstoy's edicts had been executed,
all memorials to Poushkin would have

disappeared ; chiefly because of the poet's addiction to the eternal female. In such a case Tolstoy is implacable. He admits the the kind of love whose object is the establishing of a family, but no more. Don Juan is a hateful transgressor. Think of Levin, and his attitude to prostitutes. He is exasperated, indignant, even forgets the need for compassion, and calls them "beasts." In the eternal female Tolstoy sees temptation, seduction, sin, *great danger*. Therefore it is necessary to keep quite away from the danger. But surely danger is the dragon which guards every treasure on earth. And again, no matter what his precautions, a man will meet his fate sooner or later, and come into conflict with the dragon. Surely this is an axiom. Poushkin and Lermontov loved danger, and therefore sought women. They paid a heavy price, but while they lived they lived freely and lightly. If they had cared to peep in the book of destinies, they might have averted or avoided their sad end. But they preferred to trust their star—lucky or unlucky. Tolstoy was the first among us—we cannot speak of Gogol—who began to fear life. He was the first to start open moralising. In so far as public opinion and personal dignity demand it, he did go to meet his dangers : but not a step further. So he avoided women, art, and philosophy. Love *per se*, that is, love which does not lead to a family, like wisdom *per se*, which is wisdom that has no utilitarian motive, and like art for art's sake, seemed to him the worst of temptations, leading to the destruction of the soul. When he plunged too deep in thinking, he was seized with panic. " It seemed to me I was going mad, so I went away to the Bashkirs for koumiss." Such confessions are common in his works. And surely there is no other way with temptations, than to cut short, at once, before it is too late. Tolstoy preserved himself on account of his inborn instinct for departing betimes from a dangerous situation. Save for this cautious prompting he would probably have ended like Lermontov or Poushkin. True, he might have gone deeper into nature, and revealed us rare secrets, instead of preaching at us abstinence, humility, simplicity and so on. But such luck fell to the fate of Dostoevsky. Dostoevsky had very muddled relations with morality. He was too racked by disease and circumstance to get much profit out of the rules of morality. The hygiene of the soul,

like that of the body, is beneficial only
to healthy men. To the sick it is simply
harmful. The more Dostoevsky engaged
himself with high morality, the more in-
extricably entangled he became. He wanted
to respect the personality in a woman,
and only the personality, and so he came
to the point where he could not look on
any woman, however ugly, with indifference.
The elder Karamazov and his affair with
Elizabeth Smerdyascha (Stinking Lizzie)—
in what other imagination could such a
union have been contemplated? Dostoevsky,
of course, reprimands Karamazov, and thanks
to the standards of modern criticism, such
a reprimand is accounted sufficient to
exonerate our author. But there are other
standards. If a writer sets out to tell you
that no drab could be so loathsome that
her ugliness would make you forget she was
woman; and if for illustration of this novel
idea we are told the history of Fiodov
Karamazov with the deformed, repulsive
idiot, Stinking Lizzie; then, in face of
such "imaginative art" it is surely out
of place to preserve the usual confidence
in that writer. We do not speak of the
interest and *appreciation* of Dostoevsky's
tastes and ideas. Not for one moment will

I assert that those who with Poushkin and Lermontov can see the Eternal Female only in young and charming women, have any advantage over Dostoevsky. Of course, we are not forbidden to live according to our tastes, and we may, like Tolstoy, call certain women "beasts." But who has given us the right to assert that we are higher or better than Dostoevsky? Judging "objectively," all the points go to show that Dostoevsky is better—at any rate he saw further, deeper. He could find an original interest, he could discover *das ewig Weibliche* where we should see nothing of attraction at all, where Goethe would avert his face. Stinking Lizzie is not a beast, as Levin would say, but a woman who is able, if even for a moment, to arouse a feeling of love in a man. And we thought she was worse than nothing, since she roused in us only disgust. Dostoevsky made a discovery, we with our refined feelings missed it. His distorted, abnormal sense showed a greater sensitiveness, in which our high morality was deficient. . . . And the road to the great truth this time, as ever, is through deformity. Idealists will not agree. They are quite justly afraid that one may not reach the truth, but may get stuck in the mud. Idealists are careful men, and not nearly so stupid as their ideals would lead us to suppose.

8

New ideas, even our own, do not quickly conquer our sympathies. We must first get accustomed to them.

9

A point of view.—Every writer, thinker—even every educated person thinks it necessary to have a permanent point of view. He climbs up some elevation and never climbs down again all his days. Whatever he sees from this point of view, he believes to be reality, truth, justice, good—and what he does not see he excludes from existence. Man is not much to blame for this. Surely there is no very great joy in moving from point of view to point of view, shifting one's camp from peak to peak. We have no wings, and "a winged thought" is only a nice metaphor—unless, of course, it refers to logical thinking. There to be sure great volatility is usual, a lightness which comes from perfect naïveté, if not ignorance. He who really wishes to know something, and not merely to have a philosophy, does not rely on logic and is not allured by reason. He must clamber from summit to summit, and, if necessary, hibernate in the dales. For a wide horizon leads to illusions, and in order to familiarise oneself with any object, it is essential to go close up to it, touch it, feel it, examine it from top to bottom and on every side. One must be ready, should this be impossible otherwise, to sacrifice the customary position of the body : to wriggle, to lie flat, to stand on one's head, in a word, to assume the most unnatural of attitudes. Can there be any question of a permanent point of view ? The more mobility and elasticity a man has, the less he values the ordinary equilibrium of his body; the oftener he changes his outlook, the more he will take in. If, on the other hand, he imagines that from this or the other pinnacle he has the most comfortable survey of the world and life, leave him alone; he will never know anything. Nay, he does not want to know, he cares more about his personal convenience than about the quality of his work. No doubt he will attain to fame and success, and thus brilliantly justify his "point of view."

10

Fame.—" A thread from everyone, and the naked will have a shirt." There is no beggar but has his thread of cotton, and he will not grudge it to a naked man—no, nor even to a fully dressed one; but will bestow it on the first comer. The poor, who want to forget their poverty, are very ready with their threads. Moreover, they prefer to give them to the rich, rather than to a fellow-tramp. To load the rich with benefits, must not one be very rich indeed ? That is why fame is so easily got. An ambitious person asks admiration and respect from the crowd, and is rarely denied. The mob feel that their throats are their own, and their arms are strong. Why not vociferate and clap, seeing that you can turn the head not only of a beggar like yourself, but of a future hero, God knows how almighty a person. The humiliated citizen who has hitherto been hauled off to the police station if he shouted, suddenly feels that his throat has acquired a new value. Never before has anyone given a rap for his worthless opinion, and now seven cities are ready to quarrel for it, as for the right to claim Homer. The citizen is delighted, he shouts at the top of his voice, and is ready to throw

all his possessions after his shouts. So the
hero is satisfied. The greater the shout,
the deeper his belief in himself and his
mission. What will a hero not believe!
For he forgets so soon the elements of which
his fame and riches are made. Heroes
usually are convinced that they set out on
their noble career, not to beg shouts from
beggars, but to heap blessings on mankind.
If they could only call to mind with what
beating hearts they awaited their first
applause, their first alms, how timidly they
curried favour with ragged beggars, perhaps
they would speak less assuredly of their
own merits. But our memory is fully
acquainted with Herbert Spencer and his
law of adaptability, and thus many a worthy
man goes gaily on in full belief in his own
stupendous virtue.

II

In defence of righteousness.—Inexperienced
and ingenuous people see in righteousness
merely a burden which lofty people have
assumed out of respect for law or for some
other high and inexplicable reason. But
a righteous man has not only duties but
rights. True, sometimes, when the law is
against him, he has to compromise. Yet
how rarely does the law desert him! No

cruelty matters in him, so long as he does not infringe the statutes. Nay, he will ascribe his cruelty as a merit to himself, since he acts out of no personal considerations, but in the name of sacred justice. No matter what he may do, once he is sanctioned he sees in his actions only merit, merit, merit. Modesty forbids him to say too much—but if he were to let go, what a luxurious panegyric he might deliver to himself! Remembering his works, he praises himself at all times; not aloud, but inwardly. The nature of virtue demands it: man must rejoice in his morality and ever keep it in mind. And after that, people declare that it is hard to be righteous. Whatever the other virtues may be, certainly righteousness has its selfish side. As a rule it is decidedly worth while to make considerable sacrifices in order later on to enjoy in calm confidence all that surety and those rights bestowed on a man by morality and public approval. Look at a German who has paid his contribution to a society for the assistance of the indigent. Not one stray farthing will he give, not to a poor wretch who is starving before his eyes. And in this he feels right. This is righteousness out and out: pay your tax and enjoy the

162

privileges of a high-principled man. So
righteousness is much in vogue with cultured, commercial nations. Russians have
not quite got there. They are afraid of
the exactions of righteousness, not guessing
the enormous advantages derived. A Russian has a permanent relationship with
his conscience, which costs him far more
than the most moral German, or even
Englishman, has to pay for his righteousness.

12

The best way of getting rid of tedious,
played-out truths is to stop paying them the
tribute of respect and to treat them with a
touch of easy familiarity and derision. To
put into brackets, as Dostoevsky did, such
words as good, self-sacrifice, progress, and
so on, will alone achieve you much more
than many brilliant arguments would do.
Whilst you still contest a certain truth, you
still believe in it, and this even the least
penetrating individual will perceive. But
if you favour it with no serious attention,
and only throw out a scornful remark now
and then, the result is different. It is
evident you have ceased to be afraid of the
old truth, you no longer respect it. And
this sets people thinking.

13

Four walls.—Arm-chair philosophy is being condemned—rightly. An arm-chair thinker is busy deciding on everything that is taking place in the world : the state of the world market, the existence of a world-soul, wireless telegraphy and the life after death, the cave dweller and the perfectibility of man, and so on and so on. His chief business is so to select his statements that there shall be no internal contradiction ; and this will give an appearance of truth. Such work, which is quite amusing and even interesting, leads at last to very poor results. Surely verisimilitudes of truth are not truth : nor have necessarily anything in common with truth. Again, a man who undertakes to talk of everything probably knows nothing. Thus a swan can fly, and walk, and swim. But it flies indifferently, walks badly, and swims poorly. An arm-chair philosopher, enclosed by four walls, sees nothing but those four walls, and yet of these precisely he does not choose to speak. If by accident he suddenly realised them and spoke of them his philosophy might acquire an enormous value. This may happen when a study is converted into a prison : the same four walls, but impossible not to think of them! Whatever the prisoner turns his mind to—Homer, the Greek-Persian wars, the future world-peace, the bygone geological cataclysms—still the four walls enclose it all. The calm of the study supplanted by the pathos of imprisonment. The prisoner has no more contact with the world, and no less. But now he no longer slumbers and has grayish dreams called world-conceptions. He is wide awake and strenuously living. His philosophy is worth hearing. But man is not distinguished for his powers of discrimination. He sees solitude and four walls, and says: a study. He dreams of the market-place, where there is noise and jostling, physical bustle, and decides that there alone life is to be met. He is wrong as usual. In the market-place, among the crowd, do not men sleep their deadest sleep? And is not the keenest spiritual activity taking place in seclusion?

14

The Spartans made their helots drunk as an example and warning to their noble youths. A good method, no doubt, but what are we of the twentieth century to do? Whom shall we make drunk? We have no slaves, so we have instituted a higher literature. Novels and stories describe drunken, dissolute men, and paint them in such horrid colours that every reader feels all his desire for vice depart from him. Unfortunately only our Russians are either too conscientious or not sufficiently rectilinear in their minds. Instead of showing the drunken helot as an object of repugnance, as the Spartans did, they try to describe vice truthfully. Realism has taken hold. Indeed, why make a fuss ? What does it matter if the writer's description is a little more or less ugly than the event ? Was justice invented that everything, *even evil*, should be kept intact ? Surely evil must be simply rooted out, banned, placed outside the pale. The Spartans did not stand on ceremony with living men, and yet our novelists are afraid of being unjust to imaginary drunken helots. And, so to speak, out of humane feeling too. . . . How naïve one must be to accept such a justification ! Yet everybody accepts it. Tolstoy alone, towards the end, guessed that humanitarianism is only a pretext in this case, and that we Russians have described vice not only for the purpose of scaring our readers. In modern masters the word vice arouses not disgust, but insatiable curiosity.

Perhaps the wicked thing has been persecuted in vain, like so many other good
things. Perhaps it should have been studied,
perhaps it held mysteries. . . . On the
strength of this "perhaps" morality was
gradually abandoned, and Tolstoy remained
almost alone in his indignation. Realism
reigns, and a drunken helot arouses envy
in timid readers who do not know where to
put their trust, whether in the traditional
rules or in the appeal of the master. A
drunken helot an ideal! What have we
come to ? Were it not better to have stuck
to Lycurgus ? Have we not paid too dearly
for our progress ?

Many people think we have paid too
dearly—not to mention Tolstoy, who
is now no longer taken quite seriously,
though still accounted a great man. Any
mediocre journalist enjoys greater influence
than this master-writer of the Russian land.
It is inevitable. Tolstoy insists on thinking about things which are nobody's concern.
He has long since abandoned this world—
and does he continue to exist in any other ?
Difficult question! "Tolstoy writes books
and letters, therefore he exists." This
inference, once so convincing, now has
hardly any effect on us : particularly if we

take into account what it is that Tolstoy writes. In several of his last letters he expresses opinions which surely have no meaning for an ordinary man. They can be summed up in a few words. Tolstoy professes an extreme egoism, sollipsism, solus-ipse-ism. That is, in his old age, after infinite attempts to love his neighbour, he comes to the conclusion that not only is it impossible to love one's neighbour, but that there *is* no neighbour, that in all the world Tolstoy alone exists, that there is even no world, but only Tolstoy: a view so obviously absurd, that it is not worth refuting. By the way, there is also no possibility of refuting it, unless you admit that logical inferences are non-binding. Sollipsism dogged Tolstoy already in early youth, but at that time he did not know what to do with the impertinent, oppressive idea, so he ignored it. Finally, he came to it. The older a man becomes, the more he learns how to make use of impertinent ideas. Fairly recently Tolstoy could pronounce such a dictum: "Christ taught men not to do stupid things." Who but Tolstoy could have ventured on such an interpretation of the gospels? Why have we all held—all of us but Tolstoy—that these words contained the greatest blasphemy on Christ and His teaching? But it was Tolstoy's last desperate attempt to save himself from sollipsism, without at the same time flying in the face of logic: even Christ appeared among men only to teach them common sense. Whence follows that "mad" thoughts may be rejected with an easy conscience, and the advantage, as usual, remains with the wholesome, reasonable, sensible thoughts. There is room for good and for reason. Good is self-understood; it need not be explained. If only good existed in the world, there would exist no questions, neither simple nor ultimate. This is why youth never questions. What indeed should it question: the song of the nightingale, the morning of May, happy laughter, all the predicates of youth? Do these need interpretation? On the contrary, any explanation is reduced to these The proper questions arise only on contact with evil. A hawk struck a nightingale, flowers withered, Boreas froze laughing youth—and in terror our questions arose. "That is evil. The ancients were right. Not in vain is our earth called a vale of tears and sorrow." And once questions are started, it is impossible and unseemly to hurry the answers,

still less anticipate the questions. The
nightingale is dead and will sing no longer,
the listener is frozen to death and can hear
no more songs. The situation is so palp-
ably absurd that only with the intention of
getting rid of the question at any cost will
one strive for a sensible answer. The
answer must be absurd—if you don't want
it, don't question. But if you must question,
then be ready beforehand to reconcile
yourself with something like sollipsism or
modern realism. Thought is in a dilemma,
and dare not take the leap to get out.
We laugh at philosophy, and, as long
as possible, avoid evil. But nearly all
men feel the intolerable cramp of such a
situation, and each at his risk ventures to
swim to shore on some more or less witty
theory. A few courageous ones speak the
truth—but they are neither understood nor
respected. When a man's words show the
depth of the pain through which he has
passed, he is not, indeed, condemned, but
the world begins to talk of his tragic state
of soul, and to take on a mournful look
fitting to the occasion. Others more scrupulous feel that phrases and mournful looks
are unfitting, yet they cannot dwell at
length on the tragedies of outsiders, so they

170

take on an exaggeratedly stern bearing, as if to say, "We feel deeply, but we do not wish to show our feeling." They really feel nothing, only want to make others believe how sensitive and modest they are. At times this leads to curious results, even in writers of the first order of renown. Thus Anatole France, the inventor of that most charming smile which is intended to convince men that he feels everything and understands everything, but does not cry out, because that would not be fitting, in one of his novels takes upon himself the noble rôle of advocate of the victims of a crime, against the criminal. "Our time," he says, "out of *pity* to the criminal forgets the sufferings of his victim." This, I repeat, is one of the most curious misrepresentations of modern endeavour. It is true we in Russia talk a good deal about compassion, particularly to criminals, and Anatole France is by no means the only man who thinks that our distinguishing characteristic is extreme sensitiveness and tender-heartedness. But as a matter of fact the modern man who thinks for himself is not drawn to the criminal by a sense of compassion, which would incontestably be better applied to the victim, but by curiosity, or if you like, inquisitiveness. For thousands of years man has sought to solve the great mystery of life through a God-conception—with theodicy and metaphysical theories as a result, both of which deny the possibility of a mystery. Theodicy has long ago wearied us. The mechanistic theories, which contend that there is nothing special in life, that its appearance and disappearance depend on the same laws as those of the conservation of energy and the indestructibility of matter, these look more plausible at first sight, but people do not take to them. And no theory can survive men's reluctance to believe in it. In a word, good has not justified the expectations placed on it. Reason has done no better. So overwrought mankind has turned from its old idols and enthroned madness and evil. The smiling Anatole argues, and proves—proves excellently. But who does not know what his proofs amount to ?—and who wants them ? It may be our children will take fright at the task we have undertaken, will call us " squandering parents," and will set themselves again to heaping up treasures, spiritual and material. Again they will believe in ideals, progress, and such like. For my own part, I have hardly any doubt of it.

Sollipsism and the cult of groundlessness are not lasting, and, most of all, they are not to be handed down. The final triumph, in life as in old comedies, rests with goodness and common sense. History has known many epochs like ours, and gone through with them. Degeneration follows on the heels of immoderate curiosity, and sweeps away all refined and exaggerately well-informed individuals. Men of genius have no posterity—or their children are idiots. Not for nothing is nature so majestically serene: she has hidden her secrets well enough. Which is not surprising, considering how unscrupulous she is. No despot, not the greatest villain on earth, has ever wielded power with the cruelty and heartlessness of nature. The least violation of her laws—and the severest punishment follows. Disease, deformity, madness, death —what has not our common mother contrived to keep us in subjection? True, certain optimists think that nature does not punish us, but educates us. So Tolstoy sees it. "Death and sufferings, like animated scarecrows, boo at man and drive him into the one way of life open to him: for life is subject to its own law of reason." Not a bad method of upbringing. Exactly

173

like using wolves and bears. Unfortunate man, bolting from one booing monster, is not always able in time to dodge into the one correct way, and dashes straight into the maw of another beast of prey. Then what ? And this often happens. Without disparagement of the optimists, we may say that sooner or later it happens to every man. After which no more running. You won't tear yourself out of the claws of madness or disease. Only one thing is left : in spite of traditions, theodicy, wiseacres, and most of all in spite of oneself, to go on praising mother nature and her great goodness. Let future generations reject us, let history stigmatise our names, as the names of traitors to the human cause —still we will compose hymns to deformity, destruction, madness, chaos, darkness. And after that—let the grass grow.

15

Astrology and alchemy lived their day and died a natural death. But they left a posterity—chemistry inventing dyes, and astronomy accumulating formulae. So it is. Geniuses beget idiots : especially when the mothers are very virtuous, as in this case,

when their virtue is extraordinary. For the
mothers are public utility and morality.
The alchemists wasted their time seeking
the philosopher's stone; the astrologers.
swindled people telling fortunes by the
stars. Wedded to utility these two fathers
have begotten the chemists and astronomers.
. . . Nobody will dispute the genealogy.
Perhaps even none will dispute that, from
idiotic children one may, with a measure of
probability, infer genius in the parents.
There are certain indications that this is
so—though of course one may not go beyond
supposition. But supposition is enough.
There are more arguments in store. For
instance—our day is so convinced of the
absolute nonsense and uselessness of alchemy
and astrology that no one dreams of
verifying the conviction. We know there
were many charlatans and liars amongst
alchemists and astrologers. But what does
this prove? In every department there
are the same mediocre creatures who speculate on human credulity. However positive
our science of medicine is, there are many
fraudulent doctors who rob their patients.
The alchemists and astrologers were, in all
probability, the most remarkable men of
their time. I will go further: in spite of

dye-stuffs and formulae, even in our nine-teenth century, which was so famous for its inventions and discoveries, the most eminent, talented men still sought the philosopher's stone and forecast the destinies of man. And those among them who were possessed of a poetic gift won universal attention. In the old days, *consensu sapientium*, a poet was allowed all kinds of liberties: he might speak of fate, miracles, spirits, the life beyond—indeed of anything, provided he was interesting. That was enough. The nineteenth century paid its tribute to restlessness. Never were there so many disturbing, throbbing writers as during the epoch of telephones and tele-graphs. It was held indecent to speak in plain language of the vexed and troubled aspirations of the human spirit. Those guilty of the indecency were even dosed with bromides and treated with shower-baths and concentrated foods. But all this is external, it belongs to a history of "fashions" and cannot interest us here. The point is that alchemy and astrology did not die, they only shammed death and left the stage for a time. Now, apparently, they are tired of seclusion and are coming forward again, having pushed their unsuccessful children into the background. Well, so be it. *A la bonne heure!* . . .

16

Man comes to the pass where all experience seems exhausted. Wherever he go, whatever he see, all is old and wearyingly familiar. Most people explain this by saying that they really know everything, and that from what they have experienced they can infer all experience. This phase of the exhaustion of life usually comes to a man between thirty-five and forty —the best period, according to Karamzin. Not seeing anything new, the individual assumes he is completely matured and has the right to judge of everything. Knowing what has been he can forecast what will be. But Karamzin was mistaken about the best period, and the " mature " people are mistaken about the " nothing new can happen." The fact of spiritual stagnation should not be made the ground for judging all life's possibilities from known possibilities. On the contrary, such stagnation should prove that however rich and multifarious the past may have been, it has not exhausted a tittle of the whole possibilities. From that which has been it is impossible to infer what will be. Moreover, it is unnecessary—except, perhaps, to give us a sense of our full maturity and let us enjoy all the charms of the best period of life, so eloquently described by Karamzin. The temptation is not overwhelming. So that, if man is under the necessity of enduring a period of arrest and stagnation, and until such time as life re-starts is doomed to meditation, would it not be better to use this meditating *interregnum* for a directly opposite purpose from the one indicated: that is to say, for the purpose of finding in our past signs which tell us that the future has every right to be anything whatsoever, like or utterly unlike the past. Such signs, given a good will to find them, may be seen in plenty. At times one comes to the conclusion that the natural connection of phenomena, as hitherto observed, is not at all inevitable for the future, and that miracles which so far have seemed impossible, may come to seem possible, even natural, far more natural than that loathsome law of sequence, the law of the regularity of phenomena. We are bored stiff with regularity and sequence—confess it, you also, you men of science. At the mere thought that, however we may think, we can get no further than the acknowledgment of

178

the old regularity, an invincible disgust
to any kind of mental work overcomes us.
To discover another law—still another—
when already we have far more than we
can do with! Surely if there is any will-
to-think left in us, it is established in the
supposition that the mind cannot and must
not have any bounds, any limits; and
that the theory of knowledge, which is
based on the *history* of knowledge and on a
few very doubtful assumptions, is only a
piece of property belonging to a certain
caste, and has nothing to do with us others
—*und die Natur zuletzt sich doch ergründe.*
What a mad impatience seizes us at times
when we realise that we shall never fathom
the great mystery! Every individual in
the world must have felt at one time the
mad desire to unriddle the universe. Even
the stodgy philosophers who invented the
theory of knowledge have at times made
surreptitious sorties, hoping to open a path
to the unknown, in spite of their own fat,
senseless books that demonstrate the advantages of scientific knowledge. Man either
lives in continuous experience, or he frees
himself from conclusions imposed by limited
experience. All the rest is the devil. From
the devil come the blandishments with

179

which Karamzin charmed himself and his readers. . . . Or is it the contrary? Who will answer! Once again, as usual, at the end of a pathetic speech one is left with a conjecture. Let every man please himself. But what about those who would like to live according to Karamzin, but cannot? I cannot speak for them. Schiller recommended hope. Will it do? To be frank, hardly. He who has once lost his peace of mind will never find it again.

17

Ever since Kant succeeded in convincing the learned that the world of phenomena is quite other than the world of true reality, and that even our own existence is not our real existence, but only the visible manifestation of a mysterious, unknown substance (substantia)—philosophy has been stuck in a new rut, and cannot move a single millimetre out of the track laid out by the great Königsbergian. Backward or forward it can go, but necessarily in the Kantian rut. For how can you get out of the counterposing of the phenomenon against the thing-in-itself? This proposition, this counterposing seems inalterable, so there is nothing left but to stick your head in the

heavy draught-collar of the theory of knowledge. Which most philosophers do, even
with a glad smile, which inevitably rouses
a suspicion that they have got what they
wanted, and their "metaphysical need"
was nothing more than a need for a harness.
Otherwise they would have kicked at the
sight of the collar. Surely the contra-
position between the world of phenomena
and the thing-in-itself is an invention of
the reasoning mind, as is the theory of
knowledge deduced from this contraposing.
Therefore the freedom-loving spirit could
reject it in the very beginning—and *basta!*
With the devil one must be very cautious.
We know quite well that if he only gets hold
of the tip of your ear he will carry off your
whole body. So it is with Reason. Grant
it one single assumption, admit but one
proposition—and *finita la commedia.* You
are in the toils. Metaphysics cannot exist
side-by-side with reason. Everything metaphysical is absurd, everything reasonable
is—positive. So we come upon a dilemma.
The fundamental predicate of metaphysics
is absurdity: and yet surely many positive
assertions can lay legitimate claim to that
self-same, highly-respectable predicate.
What then? Is there means of distin-

guishing a metaphysical absurdity from a perfectly ordinary one? May one have recourse to criteria? Will not the very criterion prove a pitfall wherein cunning reason will catch the poor man who was rushing out to freedom? There can be no two answers to this question. All services rendered by reason must be paid for sooner or later at the exorbitant price of self-renunciation. Whether you accept the assistance in the noble form of the theory of knowledge, or merely as a humble criterion, at last you will be driven forth into the streets of positivism. This happens all the time to young, inexperienced minds. They break the bridle and dash forward into space, to find themselves rushing into the same old Rome, whither, as we know, all roads lead: or, to use more lofty language, rushing into the stable whither also all roads lead. The only way to guard against positivism—granting, of course, that positivism no longer attracts your sympathies—is to cease to fear any absurdities, whether rational or metaphysical, and systematically to reject all the services of reason. Such behaviour has been known in philosophy; and I make bold to recommend it. *Credo quia absurdum* comes from the Middle Ages. Modern instances are Nietzsche and Schopenhauer. Both present noble examples of indifference to logic and common-sense: particularly Schopenhauer, who, a Kantian, even in the name of Kant made such daring sallies against reason, driving her into confusion and shame. That astounding Kantian even went so far, in the master's name still, as to attempt the overthrow of the space and time notions. He admitted clairvoyance— and to this day the learned are bothered whether to class that admission among the metaphysical or the ordinary absurdities. Really, I can't advise them. A very clever man insists on an enormous absurdity, so I am satisfied. Schopenhauer's whole campaign against intellect is very comforting. It is evident that, though he set out from the Kantian stable, he soon got sick of hauling along down the cart-ruts, and having broken the shafts, he trotted jauntily into a jungle of irreconcilable contradictions, without reflecting in the least where he was making for. The primate of will over reason; and music as the expression of our deepest essence; are not these assertions sufficient to show us how dexterously he wriggled out from the harness of synthetic judgments *a priori* which Kant had placed upon every thinker. There is indeed much more music than logic in the philosophy of Schopenhauer. Not for nothing is he excluded from the universities. But of course one may speak of him in the open; not of his ideas, naturally, but of his music. The European market is glutted with ideas. How neat and nicely-finished and logically well-turned-out those ideas are. Schopenhauer had no such goods. But what lively and splendid contradictions he boldly spreads on his stall, often even without suspicion that he ought to hide them from the police. Schopenhauer cries and laughs and gets furious or glad, without ever realising that this is forbidden to a philosopher. "Do not speak, but sing," said Zarathustra, and Schopenhauer really fulfilled the command in great measure. Philosophy may be music—though it doesn't follow that music may be called philosophy. When a man has done his work, and gives himself up to looking and listening and pleasantly accepting everything, hiding nothing from himself, then he begins to "philosophise." What good are abstract formulae to him? Why should he ask himself, before he begins to think: "What can I think about, what are the limits of

thought ? " He will think, and those who
like can do the summing up and the build-
ing of theories of knowledge. What is the
earthly use of talking about beauty ?
Beautiful things must be created. Not
one single aesthetic theory has so far been
able to guess what direction the artists'
mind will next take, or what are the limits
to his creative activity. The same with
the theory of knowledge. It may arrest
the work of a man of learning, if he be himself afraid that he is going too far, but it is
powerless to pre-determine human thought.
Even Kant's counterposing of things-in-
themselves to the world of phenomena
cannot finally clip the wings of human
curiosity. There will come a time when this
unshakeable foundation of positivism will
be shaken. All gnosiological disputes as to
what thought can or cannot achieve will
seem to our posterity just as amusing as the
disputes of the schoolmen seem to us.
" Why did they argue about the nature of
truth, when they might have gone out and
looked for truth itself ? " the future historians will ask. Let us have an answer ready
for them. Our contemporaries do not want
to go out and seek, so they make a great
deal of talk about a theory of knowledge.

18

"Trust not thyself, young dreamer."—
However sincerely you may long for truth,
whatever sufferings and horrors you may
have surpassed, do not believe your own
self, young dreamer. What you are looking
for, you won't find. At the utmost, if
you have a gift for writing you will bring
out a nice original book. Even—do not be
offended—you may be satisfied with such a
result. In Nietzsche's letters relating to
the year 1888, the year when Brandes discovered him, you will find a sad confirmation of the above. Had not Nietzsche
struggled, sought, suffered ?—and behold,
towards the end of his life, when it would
have seemed that all mundane rewards
had become trivial to him, he threw himself
with rapture on the tidings of first fame, and
rushed to share his joy with all his friends,
far and near. He does not tire of telling
in dozens of letters and in varying forms the
story of how Brandes first began his lectures
on him, Nietzsche, how the audience con-
sisted of three hundred people, and he even
quotes Brandes' placard announcement in
the original Danish. Fame just threw him
a smile, and forgotten are all the horrible
experiences of former days. The loneliness,

the desertedness, the cave in the mountain, the man into whose mouth the serpent climbed—all forgotten, every thought turned to the ordinary, easily-comprehensible good. Such is man.

Mit gier'ger Hand nach Schätzen gräbt
Und froh ist wenn er Regenwürmer findet.

19

When a man is young he writes because it seems to him he has discovered a new almighty truth which he must make haste to impart to forlorn mankind. Later, becoming more modest, he begins to doubt his truths : and then he writes to convince himself. A few more years go by, and he knows he was mistaken all round, so there is no need to convince himself. Nevertheless he continues to write, because he is not fit for any other work, and to be accounted a " superfluous " man is so horrible.

20

A very original man is often a banal writer, and vice versa. We tend so often to write not about what is going on in us, but of our *pia desideria*. Thus restless, sleepless men sing the glory of sleep and rest, which

187

have long been sung to death. And those who sleep ten hours on end and are always up to the mark must perforce dream about adventures and storms and dangers, and even extol everything problematical.

21

When one reads the books of long-dead men, a strange sensation comes over one. These men who lived two hundred, three hundred, three thousand years ago are so far off now from this writing which they have left on earth. Yet we look for eternal truths in their works.

22

The truth which I have the right to announce so solemnly to-day, even to the first among men, will probably be a stale old lie on my lips to-morrow. So I will deprive myself of the right of calling such a truth my own. Probably I shall deprive no one but myself: others will go on loving and praising the self-same truth, living with it.

23

A writer who cannot lie with inspiration—and that is a great art, which few may accomplish—loves to make an exhibition

of honesty and frankness.   Nothing else is
left him to do.

24

The source of originality.—A man who
has lost all hope of rooting out of himself a
certain radical defect of character, or even
of hiding the flaw from others, turns round
and tries to find in his defect a certain merit.
If he succeeds in convincing his acquaint-
ances, he achieves a double gain: first,
he quiets his conscience, and then he acquires
a reputation for being original.

25

Men begin to strive towards great ends
when they feel they cannot cope with the
little tasks of life.   They often have their
measure of success.

26

A belch interrupts the loftiest meditation.
You may draw a conclusion if you like:
if you don't like, you needn't.

27

A woman of conviction.—We forgive a
man his "convictions," however unwillingly.
It goes without saying that we balk at
any individual who believes in his own

infallibility, but one must reconcile oneself with necessity. It is ugly and preposterous to have corns on one's hands, but still, they can't be avoided in this unparadisal earth of sweat and labour. But why see an ideal in callosities ? In practical life, particularly in the social political life to which we are doomed, convictions are a necessity. Unity is strength, and unity is possible only among people who think alike. Again, a deep conviction is in itself a strong force, far more powerful than the most logical argumentation. Sometimes one has only to pronounce in a full, round, vibrating chest voice, such as is peculiar to people of conviction, some trifling sentence, and an audience hitherto unconvinced is carried away. Truth is often dumb, particularly a new truth, which is most shy of people, and which has a feeble, hoarse voice. But in certain situations that which will influence the crowd is more important than that which is genuine truth. Convictions are necessary to a public man; but he who is too clever to believe in himself entirely, and is not enough of an actor to look as if he believed, he had best give up public work altogether. At the same time he will realise that lack of

convictions is not profitable, and will look
with more indulgence on such as are bound
to keep themselves well supplied. Yet
all the more will he dislike those men who
without any necessity disfigure themselves
with the coarse tattoo marks. And
particularly he will object to such women.
What can be more intolerable than a woman
of conviction. She lives in a family, without
having to grind for her daily bread—why
disfigure herself ? Why wilfully rub her
hands into corns, when she might keep
them clean and pretty ! Women, moreover,
usually pick up their convictions ready-
made from the man who interests them
most at the moment. And never do they
do this so vigorously as when the man
himself seems incapable of paving the way
to his ideas ! They are full of feeling for
him; they rush to the last extremities of
resource. Will not their feeble little fists
help him ? It may be touching, but in the
end it is intolerable. So it is much pleasanter
to meet a woman who believes in her
husband and does not consider it necessary
to help him. She can then dispense with
convictions.

28

Emancipation of women.—The one and only way of mastering an enemy is to learn the use of his weapons. Starting from this, modern woman, weary of being the slave of man, tries to learn all his tricks. Hard is slavery, wonderful is freedom! Slavery at last is so unendurable that a human being will sacrifice everything for freedom. Of what use are his virtues to a prisoner languishing in prison? He has one aim, one object—to get out of prison, and he values only such qualities in himself as will assist his escape. If it is necessary to break an iron grating by physical force, then strong muscles will seem to the prisoner the most desirable of all things. If cunning will help him, cunning is the finest thing on earth. Something the same happens with woman. She became convinced that man owed his priority chiefly to education and a trained mind, so she threw herself on books and universities. Learning that promises freedom is light, everything else darkness. Of course, it is a delusion, but you could never convince her of it, for that would mean the collapse of her best hopes of freedom. So that in the end woman will be as well-informed as man, she will furnish herself with broad views and unshakeable convictions, with a philosophy also—and in the end she may even learn to think logically. Then, probably, the many misunderstandings between the sexes will cease. But heavens, how tedious it will be! Men will argue, women will argue, children will probably be born fully instructed, understanding everything. With what pain will the men of the future view our women, capricious, frivolous, uninformed creatures, understanding nothing and desiring to understand nothing. A whole half of the human race neither would nor could have any understanding! But the hope lies there. Maybe we can do without understanding. Perhaps a logical mind is not an attribute, but a curse. In the struggle for existence, however, and the survival of the fittest, not a few of the best human qualities have perished. Obviously woman's illogicality is also destined to disappear. It is a thousand pities.

29

All kinds of literature are good, except the tedious, said Voltaire. We may enlarge the idea. All men and all activities are good, except the tedious. Whatever your failings and your vices, if you are only amusing or interesting all is forgiven you. Accordingly, frankness and naturalness are quite rightly considered doubtful virtues. If people say that frankness and naturalness are virtues, always take it *cum grano salis.* Sometimes it is permissible and even opportune to fire off truth of all sorts. Sometimes one may stretch oneself like a log across the road. But God forbid that such sincere practices should be raised into a principle. To out with the truth at all times, always to reveal oneself entirely, besides being impossible to accomplish, never having been accomplished even in the confessions of the greatest men, is moreover a far more risky business than it seems. I can confidently assert that if any man tried to tell the whole truth about himself, not metaphorically, for every metaphor is a covering ornament, but in plain bare words, that man would ruin himself for ever, for he would lose all interest in the eyes of his neighbours, and even in his own eyes. Each of us bears in his soul a heavy wound, and knows it, yet carries himself, *must* carry himself as if he were aware of nothing, while all around keep up the pretence. Remember Lermontov :

194

Look! around you, playfully
The crowd moves on the usual road.
Scarce a mark of trouble on the festive faces,
Not one indecent tear!
And yet is barely one amongst them
But is crushed by heavy torture,
Or has gathered the wrinkles of young age
Save from crime or loss.

These words are horribly true—and the
really horrible should be concealed, it
frightens one off. I admit, Byron and
Lermontov could make it alluring. But
all that is alluring depends on vagueness,
remoteness. Any monster may be beautiful
in the distance. And no man can be interesting unless he keep a certain distance between
himself and people. Women do not understand this. If they like a man, they try
to come utterly near to him, and are surprised that he does not meet their frankness
with frankness, and admit them to his holy
of holies. But in the innermost sanctuary
the only beauty is inaccessibility. As a rule
it is not a sanctuary but a lair where the
wounded beast in man has run to lick his
wounds. And shall this be done in public?
People generally, and women particularly,
ought to be given something positive. In

books one may still sing the praise of wounds, hopelessness, and despair—whatever you like, for books are still literature, a conventionality. But to strip one's anguish in the open market, to confess an incurable disease to others, this is to kill one's soul, not to relieve it. All, even the best men, have some aversion for you. Perhaps in the interest of order and decorum they will grant you a not-too-important place in their philosophy of life. For in a philosophy of life, as in a cemetery, a place is prepared for each and all, and everyone is welcome. There also are enclosures where rubbish is dumped to rot. But for those who have as yet no desire to be fitted into a world-philosophy, I would advise them to keep their tongue between their teeth, or like Nietzsche and Dostoevsky, take to literature. To a writer, in books and only in books, all is permitted provided he has talent. But in actual living even a writer must not let loose too much, lest people should guess that in his books he is telling the truth.

30

Poushkin asserts that the poet himself can and must be the judge of his own work. "Are you content, exacting artist ? Content, then let the mob revile." It is needless to argue against this, for how could you prove that the supreme verdict belongs not to the poet himself, but to public opinion? Nor, for that matter, can we prove Poushkin right. We must agree or disagree, as we like. But we cannot reject the evidence. Whether you like it or not, Poushkin was evidently satisfied with his own work, and did not need his reader's sanction. Happy man! And it seems to me he owed his happiness exclusively to his inability to pass beyond certain limits. I doubt if all poets would agree to repeat Poushkin's verse quoted above. I decidedly refuse to believe that Shakespeare, for instance, after finishing *Hamlet* or *King Lear* could have said to himself: "I, who judge my work more strictly than any other can judge, am satisfied." I do not think he can even have thought for a moment of the merits of his works, *Hamlet* or *King Lear*. To Shakespeare, after Hamlet, the word " satisfied " must have lost all its meaning, and if he used it, it was only by force of habit, as we sometimes call to a dead person. His own works must have seemed to him imperfect, mean, pitiful, like the sob of a child or the moaning of a sick man. He gave

197

them to the theatre, and most probably was surprised that they had any success. Perhaps he was glad that his tears were of some use, if only for amusing and instructing people. And probably in this sense the verdict of the crowd was dearer to him than his own verdict. He could not help accusing his own offspring—thank heaven, other people acquitted it. True, they acquitted it because they did not understand, or understood imperfectly, but this did not matter. "Use every man after his desert, and who should 'scape a whipping ?" asked Hamlet. Shakespeare knew that a strict tribunal would reject his works : for they contain so many terrible questions, and not one perfect answer. Could anyone be "satisfied" at that rate ? Perhaps with *Comedy of Errors, Twelfth Night,* or even *Richard III.*—but after *Hamlet* a man may find rest only in his grave. To speak the whole truth, I doubt if Poushkin himself maintained the view we have quoted till the end of his days, or even if he spoke all he felt when he wrote the poem in 1830. Possibly he felt how little a poet can be satisfied with his work, but pride prevented his admitting it, and he tried to console himself with his superiority over the crowd.

Which is undeniably a right thing to do.
Insults—and Poushkin had to endure many
—are answered with contempt; and woe
to the poor wretch who feels impelled to
justify his contempt by his own merits,
according to the stern voice of conscience.
Such niceness is dangerous and unnecessary.
If a man would preserve his strength and
his confidence he must give up magnanimity,
he must learn to despise people, and even if
he cannot despise them he must have the
air of one who would not give a pin's head
for anybody. He must appear always content. . . . Poushkin was a clever man and
a deep nature.

31

Metaphysics against their will.—It often
occurs to us that evil is not altogether so
unnecessary, after all. Diseases, humilia-
tions, miseries, deformity, failure, and all
the rest of those plants which flourish with
such truly tropical luxuriance on our planet,
are probably essential to man. Poets sing
plentifully of sorrow.

"*Nous sommes les apprentis, la douleur
est notre maître,*" said de Musset. On this
subject everybody can bring forth a quota-
tion, not only from the philosophers, who
are a cold, heartless tribe, but from tender,

gentle, or sentimental poets. Doubtless
one knows many instances where suffering
has profited a man. True also, one knows
many cases of the direct opposite. And these
are all cases of profound, earnest, outrageous,
incredibly outrageous suffering. Look at
Tchekhov's men and women—plainly drawn
from life, or at any rate, exceedingly life-
like. Uncle Vanya, an old man of fifty,
cries beside himself all over the stage,
" My life is done for, my life is done for,"
and senselessly shoots at a harmless professor. The hero in *A Tedious Story* was
a quiet, happy man engaged in work of
real importance, when suddenly a horrible
disease stole upon him, not killing him, but
taking him between its loathsome jaws.
But what for ? Then Tchekhov's girls and
women ! They are mostly young, innocent,
fascinating. And always there lies in wait
for them round every corner a meaningless,
rude, ugly misery which murders even the
most modest hopes. They sob bitterly, but
fate takes no notice. How explain such
horrors ? Tchekhov is silent. He does not
weep himself—he left off long ago, and
besides it is a humiliating thing for a grown-
up person to do. Setting one's teeth, it is
necessary either to keep silent or—to explain.

Well, metaphysics undertakes the explanation. Where common sense stops, metaphysics must take another stride. "We have seen," it says, "many instances where at first glance suffering seemed absurd and needless, but where later on a profound significance was revealed. Thus it may be that what we cannot explain may find its explanation in time. 'Life is lost,' cries Uncle Vanya, 'Life is done for,' repeat the voices of girls innocently perishing—yet nothing is lost. The very horror which a drowning man experiences goes to show that the drowning is nothing final. It is only the beginning of greater events. The less a man has fulfilled in experience, the more in him remains of unsatisfied passion and desire, the greater are the grounds for thinking that his essence cannot be destroyed, but must manifest itself somehow or other in the universe. Voluntary asceticism and self-denial, such common human phenomena, help to solve the riddle. Nobody compels a man, he imposes suffering and abstinence on himself. It is an incomprehensible instinct, but still an instinct which, rooted in the depths of our nature, prompts us to a decision repugnant to reason : renounce life, save yourself. The majority of men do not hear or do not heed the prompting. And then nature, which cannot rely on our sensibility, has recourse to violence. She shows glimpses of Paradise to us in our youth, awakens hopes and impossible desires, and at the moment of our supreme expectation she shows us the hollowness of our hope. Nearly every life can be summed up in a few words : man was shown heaven—and thrown into the mud. We are all ascetics —voluntary or involuntary. Here on earth dreams and hopes are only awakened, not fulfilled. And he who has endured most suffering, most privation, will awaken in the afterwards most keenly alive." Such long speeches metaphysics whispers to us. And we repeat them, often leaving out the " it may be." Sometimes we believe them, and forge our philosophies from them. Even we go so far as to assert that had we the power we would change nothing, absolutely nothing in the world. And yet, if by some miracle such power came into our hands, how triumphantly we would send to the devil all philosophies and lofty world-conceptions, all ideals and metaphysics, and plainly and simply, without reflection, abolish sufferings, deformities, failures, all those things to which we attach such a high

educational value, abolish them from the
face of the earth. We are fed up, oh, how
fed up we are with carrying on our studies.
But it can't be helped. *Faute de mieux,*
let us keep on inventing systems, thinking
them out. But let us agree not to be cross
with those who don't want to have anything
to do with our systems. Really, they have
a perfect right.

32

Old age must be respected—so all say,
even the old. And the young willingly
meet the demand. But in such spontaneous,
even often emphatic respect, is there not
something insulting to old age. Every
young man, by his voluntary deference,
seems to say: " And still the rising star
shines brighter than the setting." And
the old, accepting the respect, are well
aware that they can count on nothing more.
The young are attentive and respectful to
the old only upon the express condition
that the latter shall behave like old people,
and stand aside from life. Let a real man
try to follow Faust's example, and what a
shindy there will be! The old, being as a
rule helpless, are compelled to bow to public
opinion and behave as if their only interests

were the interests of righteousness, good name, and such-like Platonic attributes. Only a few go against the convention, and these are monsters and degenerates. We do not wish old men to have desires, so that life is arranged as if old men desired nothing. This, of course, is no great matter : even the young are compelled to be satisfied with less than nothing, in our system. We are not out to meddle with human rights. Our point is that science and philosophy take enforced appearances for reality. Grey hair is supposed to be a sure sign of victory over the passions. Hence, seeing that we must all come to grey hairs, therefore the ultimate business of man is to overcome the passions. . . . On this granite foundation whole systems of philosophy are built. It is not worth while quarrelling with a custom—let us continue to pay respect to old age. But let us look in other directions for philosophic bases. It is time to open a free road to the passions even in the province of metaphysics.

33

Dostoevsky — advocatus diaboli. — Dostoevsky, like Nietzsche, disliked Protestantism, and tried every means of degrading

it in the eyes of the world. As normally
he was not over scrupulous, it is probable
he never took the trouble to acquaint himself with Luther's teaching. His flair did
not deceive him : the Protestant religion
and morality was most unsuitable to him
and his kind. But does this mean that it
was to be calumniated, and judged, as
Dostoevsky judged it, merely by the etymo-
logical meaning of a word ? Protestant—a
protester, one who only protests and has no
positive content. A child's text-book of
history will show the absurdity of the defini-
tion. Protestantism is, on the whole, the
most positive, *assertive* creed of all the
Christian religions. It certainly protested
against Catholicism, but against the destructive tendencies in the latter, and in the
name of positive ideals. Catholicism relied
too much on its power and its spell, and
most of all on the infallibility of its dogmas
to which it offered millions of victims. To
maim and mutilate a man *ad majorem
gloriam Dei* was considered a perfectly
proper thing in the Middle Ages, the period
of bloom for Catholicism. At the risk of
appearing paradoxical, I venture to assert
that ideas have been invented only for the
purpose of giving the right to mutilate

205

people. The Middle Ages nourished a mysterious, incomprehensible hatred for everything normal, self-satisfied, complete. A young, healthy, handsome man, at peace with himself, aroused suspicion and hostility in a believing Catholic. His very appearance offended religion and confuted dogma. It was not necessary to examine him. Even though he went to church, and gave no sign of doubt, either in deed or word, yet he must be a heretic, to be converted at all cost. And we know the Catholic cost: privation, asceticism, mortification of the flesh. The most normal person, kept on a monastic régime, will lose his spiritual balance, and all those virtues which belong to a healthy spirit and a healthy body. This was all Catholicism needed. It tried to obtain from people the *extreme endeavour* of their whole being. Ordinary, natural love, which found its satisfaction—this was sinful. Monks and priests were condemned to celibacy—hence monstrous and abnormal passions developed. Poverty was preached, and the most unheard-of greed appeared in the world, the more secret the stronger it became. Humility was essential—and out of bare-footed monks sprang despots who had no limits to their ambitions.

Luther was the last man to understand the meaning and value of the tasks which Catholicism had set itself. What he saw in Rome was not the accidental outcome of this or the other historical circumstance, but a result of the age-long effort of generations that had striven to attribute to life as alarming and dangerous a nature as possible. The sincere, direct, rustic German monk was too simple-minded to make out what was going on in Rome. He thought there existed one truth, and that the essence of Catholicism lay in what seemed to him an exemplary, virtuous life. He went direct to his aim ? What meaning can monasticism have ? Why deprive a priest of family happiness ? How accept the licentiousness of the pope's capital ? The common sense of the normal German revolted against the absurdity of such a state of things—and Luther neither could nor *would* see any good where common sense was utterly forgotten. The violent oscillation of life resulting from the continuous quick passage from asceticism and blind faith to unbelief and freedom of the passions aroused a mystic horror in the honest monk and released the enormous powers in him necessary to start the great struggle. How could he help protesting ?

And who was the denier, Luther, or the Rome which passed on from the keeping of the Divine Word to the arbitrary ordaining of all the mysteries of life? Luther might have forgiven the monks had they confined themselves to sophistries. But mediaeval monks had nothing in common with our philosophers. They did not look for world-conceptions in books, and logical tournaments amused them only moderately. They threw themselves into the deeps of life, they experimented on themselves and their neighbours. They passed from mortification to licentious bacchanalia. They feared nothing, spared nothing. In a word, the Rome against which Luther arose had undertaken to build Babylon again, not with stones, but with human souls. Luther, horrified, withdrew, and with him half Europe was withdrawn. That is his positive merit. And Dostoevsky attacked Lutheranism, and pitied the old catholicism and the breathless heights to which its "spiritual" children had risen. Wholesome morality and its support is not enough for Dostoevsky. All this is not "positive," it is only "protest." Whether I am believed or not, I will repeat that Vladimir Soloviov, who held that Dostoevsky was a prophet, is

208

wrong, and that N. K. Mikhailovsky, who calls him a cruel talent and a grubber after buried treasure, is right. Dostoevsky grubs after buried treasure—no doubt about that. And, therefore, it would be more becoming in the younger generation that still marches under the flag of pious idealism if, instead of choosing him as a spiritual leader, they avoided the old sorcerer, in whom only those gifted with great short-sightedness or lack of experience in life could fail to see the dangerous man.

34

It is boring and difficult to convince people, and after all, not necessary. It would be much better if every individual kept his own opinions. Unfortunately, it cannot be. Whether you like it or not, you have to admit the law of gravitation. Some people find it necessary to admit the origin of man from the monkey. In the empirical realm, however humiliating it may be, there are certain real, binding, universal truths against which no rebellion will avail. With what pleasure would we declare to a representative of science that fire does not burn, that rattlesnakes are not poisonous, that a fall from a high tower is perfectly agreeable, etc., etc., supposing he were obliged to prove to us the contrary. Unluckily the scientific person is free from the burden of proof: nature proves, and thoroughly. If nature, like metaphysics, set out to compel us through syllogisms or sermons to believe in her, how little she would get out of us. She is much more sagacious. Morality and logic she has left to Hegel and Spinoza, for herself she has taken a cudgel. Now then, try to argue against *this!* You will give in against your will. The cleverest of all the metaphysicians, Catholic inquisitors, imitated nature. They rarely tried the word, and trusted to the fire of faggots rather than of the heart. Had they only had more power, it would not be possible to find two people in the whole world disbelieving in the infallibility of the Pope. Metaphysical ideas, dreamily expecting to conquer the world by reasoned exposition, will never attain dominion. If they are bent on success, let them try more effective methods of convincing.

35

Evolution.—In recent years we see more and more change in the philosophies of writers and even of non-literary people.

The old men are beside themselves—such shiftiness seems indecent. After all, convictions are not gloves. But the young carelessly pass on from one idea to another. Irresolute men are somewhat timid, and although they abandon their former convictions they do not declare the change openly. Others, however, plainly announce, as if it were nothing, how far they now are from the beliefs they held six months ago. One even publishes whole volumes relating how he passed on from one philosophy to another, and then to a third. People see nothing alarming in that kind of " evolution." They believe it is in the ordering of things. But not so at all ! The readiness to leave off one set of convictions in order to assume another 'set shows complete indifference to convictions altogether. Not for nothing do the old sound the alarm. But to us who have fought so long against all kinds of constancy, the levity of the young is a pleasant sight. They will don materialism, positivism, Kantianism, spiritualism, and so on, one after the other, till they realise that all theories, ideas and ideals are as of little consequence as the hoopskirts and crinolines of our grandmothers. Then they will begin to live without ideals

and pre-arranged purposes, without foresight, relying on chance and their own ready
wit. This way, too, must be tried. Perhaps
we shall do better by it. . . . Anyhow, it will
be more fun.

36

Strength of will.—Weakness and paralysis
of the will, a very dangerous disease in
our times, and in most other times, consists
not in the absolute loss of desire, such as
takes place in the very old, but in the loss
of the capacity to translate desire into deed.
A diseased will is often met in violently
passionate men, so that the proverb—" Say
I will not, not I cannot "—does not always
hold good. Man often would, but cannot.
And then the force of desire instead of
moving to outward creation, works inwardly.
This is justly considered the most dangerous
effect of the weakening of the will. For
inward working is destructive working.
Man does not only, to put it scientifically,
fail to adapt nature to his needs, but he
loses his own power of adaptability to
outward circumstances. The most ordinary
doctor, or even anybody, decides that he
has before him a pathological case which
must be treated with care. The patient is

of the same opinion, whilst he still hopes. But when the treatment has had no results, the doctor draws back and speaks of the inadequacy of his science. Then what is the patient to retire upon ? It is disgusting to speak of an incurable disease. So he begins to think, think, think—all the time about things of which nobody thinks. He is gradually forgotten, and gradually he forgets everything—but first of all, that widespread truth which asserts that no judgments are valid save those that are accepted and universal. Not that he disputes the truth : he *forgets it*, and there is none to remind him. To him all his judgments seem valid and important. Of course he cannot advance the principle : let all men turn from the external world into themselves. But why advance a principle at all ? One can simply say : I am indifferent to the destinies of the external world. I do not want to move mountains or turn rivers aside or rearrange the map of Europe. I don't even want to go to the tobacconist to buy cigarettes. I don't want *to do* anything. I want to think that my inaction is the most important thing on earth, that any " disease " is better than health, and so on and so on without end. To what

213

thoughts will not a man abandoned by medicine and doctors sink down! His judgments are not binding on us, that is as clear as day. But are they uninteresting? And is that paralysis, that weakness of will, a disease only?

37

Death and metaphysics.—A superficial observer knows that the best things in life are hard to attain. Some psychologists even consider that the chief beauty of the highest things consists in their unattainability. This is surely not true—yet there is a grain in it. The roads to good things are dangerous to travel. Is it because nature is so much poorer than we imagine, so she must lock up her blessings, or is there some greater meaning in it, that we have not guessed? For the fact is, the more alluring an end we have in view, the more risks and horrors we must undertake to get there. May we not also make a contrary suggestion: that behind every danger something good is hidden, and that therefore danger serves as an indication, a mark to guide us onwards, not as a warning, as we are taught to believe. To decide this would be to decide that behind death, the greatest of dangers,

214

must lie the most promising things. It is
as well not to speculate further. We had
best stop lest we quarrel even with metaphysics. Traditional metaphysics has
always been able to illumine our temporal
existence with the reflected beams of
eternity. Let us follow the example. Let
us make no attempt to know the absolute.
If you have discovered a comforting hypothesis, even in the upper transcendental
air, drag it quickly to earth where labouring
men forever await even an imaginary relief
from their lot. We must make use of
everything, even of death, to serve the ends
of this life of ours.

38

The future.—A clever, reasonable boy,
accustomed to trust his common sense, read
in a book for children a description of a
shipwreck which occurred just as the pas-
sengers were eating their sweets at dessert.
He was astonished to learn that everyone,
women and children as well, who could
give no assistance whatever in saving the
ship, left their dessert and rushed on deck
with wailing and tears. Why wail, why
rush about, why be stupidly agitated?
The crew knew their business and would do

all that could be done. If you are going
to perish, perish you will, no matter how
you scream. It seemed to the boy that if
he had been on the ship he would just
have gone on eating his sweets to the last
moment. Justice should be done to this
judicious and irreproachable opinion. There
remained only a few minutes to live—would
it not have been better to enjoy them?
The logic is perfect, worthy of Aristotle.
And it was found impossible to prove to the
boy that he would have left his sweets,
even his favourite sweets, under the same
circumstances, and rushed and screamed
with the rest. Hence a moral—do not
decide about the future. To-day common
sense is uppermost, and sweets are your
highest law. But to-morrow you will get
rid of normality and sense, you will link
on with nonsense and absurdity, and probably you will even get a taste for bitters.
What do you think?

39

A priori *synthetic judgments.*—Kant, as
we know, found in mathematics and the
natural sciences *a priori* synthetic judgments. Was he right or wrong? Are the
judgments he indicated *a priori* or *a*

posteriori? Anyhow, one thing is certain : they are not accepted as absolutely, but only as relatively indisputable. In metaphysics, where the only curious and important truths are hidden, the case is different. Kant was compelled to admit that just where metaphysics begin the capacity of our human reason to judge *a priori* ends. But since we cannot dispense with metaphysical judgments, he proposed to substitute for them postulates. At the same time he admitted the optimistic presupposition that in the domain of the transcendental we shall find all that we miss in the world of phenomena. So that, because he could not invent a truly scientific metaphysics, he contrived to present us with a non-scientific sort. Which is to say, after many round-about journeys he brings his readers along the opposite way right back to the very spot from which he led them off. Surely non-scientific metaphysics existed before Kant : the mediaeval philosophers had plenty of phantasies and speculations, all supported by "moral" proofs. If Kant wanted to reform metaphysics, he should have got rid of its favourite method of obtaining truths through inferential "conclusions." Men are greedy, they want to

217

learn much, and get their knowledge cheap. So they think that every truth they have paid for with experience and loss of energy entitles them to a few more truths gratis: or, in philosophic language, *a priori*, by deduction. They are not ashamed to speculate with a gift that has been given them. Instead of looking, listening, touching, *seeking*, they want to infer and conclude. Certainly if they could wring any secret out of nature, no matter by what means, cunning, impudence, fraud, we would forgive them —conquerors are not judged. But nothing comes of their "conclusions" save metaphysical systems and empty prattle. It is surely time to give up conclusions, and get truth *a posteriori*, as did Shakspeare, Goethe, Dostoevsky; that is, every time you want to know anything, go and look and find out. And if one is lazy, or horrified at a new experiment, let him train himself to look on ultimate questions with indifference, as the positivists do. But moral, ontological and such like arguments!—really, it is disgusting to talk about them. Every new experiment is interesting; but our conclusions, *i.e.*, synthetic judgments *a priori*, are mostly pompous lies, not worth the scrap of paper on which they are recorded.

40

General rules.—People go to philosophers for general principles. And since philosophers are human, they are kept busy supplying the market with general principles. But what sense is there in them? None at all. Nature demands individual creative activity from us. Men won't understand this, so they wait forever for the ultimate truths from philosophy, which they will never get. Why should not every grown-up person be a creator, live in his own way at his own risk and have his own experience? Children and raw youths must go in leading strings. But adult people who want to feel the reins should be despised. They are cowards, and slothful: afraid to try, they eternally go to the wise for advice. And the wise do not hesitate to take the responsibility for the lives of others. They invent general rules, as if they had access to the sources of knowledge. What foolery! The wise are no wiser than the stupid—they have only more conceit and effrontery. Every intelligent man laughs in his soul at "bookish" views. And are not books the work of the wise? They are often extremely interesting—but only in so far as they do not contain general rules. Woe to him who would build up his life according to Hegel, Schopenhauer, Tolstoy, Schiller, or Dostoevsky. He must read them, but he must have sense, a mind of his own to live with. Those who have tried to live according to theories from books have found this out. At the best, their efforts produced banality. There is no alternative. Whether man likes or not he will at last have to realise that clichés are worthless, and that he must live from himself. There are no all-binding, universal judgments—let us manage with non-binding, non-universal ones. Only professors will suffer for it. . . .

41

Metaphysical consolations.—Metaphysics mercilessly persecutes all eudaemonistic doctrines, seeing in them a sort of *laesio majestatis* of human dignity. Our dignity forbids us to place human happiness in the highest goal. Suppose it is so ? But why then invent consolations, even metaphysical ones ? Why give to such a " pure " ideal concept as metaphysics such a coarse " sensual " partner as consolation ? —sensual in the Kantian meaning of the word. Metaphysics had much better associate herself with proud disconsolation. Consolation brings calm and ease, even quiet gratification to the soul. But surely, if metaphysics condescend to accept any assistance whatever, she must scorn all earthly gratifications, leave them to wingless positivism and materialism. What are joys and pains to metaphysics?—she is one thing, they another. Yet all of a sudden metaphysicians begin to shout about consolations. Evidently there is a misunderstanding here, and a big one. The more you pierce to the ultimate ends of the " infinite " metaphysical problems, the more finite they reveal themselves. Metaphysicians only look out for some new boon—I nearly said pleasure. Voltaire said that if there was no God, then He should be invented. We explain these words by the great Frenchman's extreme positivism. But the form only is positive, the content is purely metaphysical. All that a metaphysician wants to do is to convince himself that God exists. No matter whether he is mistaken or not, he has found a consolation. It is impossible for him to see that his belief in a certain fact does not make that fact veritable. The whole question is whether there does exist a supreme, conscious First Cause, or whether we are slaves to the laws of dead necessity. But what does the metaphysician care about this real question! Having declared himself the avowed enemy of eudaemonism, he next seeks consolation, nothing but consolation. To doubt his right to be consoled drives him to fury and madness. He is prepared to support his convictions by every means—ranging from righteous indignation to fists. It is obviously futile to try to enlighten such a creature. Once a man cares nothing for God, and seeks only to make the best of his life, you will not tear away his attention from the immediate moment. But perhaps there is a God, and neither Voltaire nor the metaphysicians have any need to invent Him. The metaphysicians never saw that an avowed disbelief in God does not prove the non-existence of God, but just the opposite; it is a surer sign of faith than ever belief is. Unfortunate metaphysicians! They might have found their greatest consolation here, and fists and moral indignation and other forms of chastisement to which they have been driven might have been spared us

42

Practical advice.—People who read much must always keep it in mind that life is one thing, literature another. Not that authors invariably lie. I declare that there are writers who rarely and most reluctantly lie. But one must know how to read, and that isn't easy. Out of a hundred book-readers ninety-nine have no idea what they are reading about. It is a common belief, for example, that any writer who sings of suffering must be ready at all times to open his arms to the weary and heavy-laden. This is what his readers feel when they read his books. Then when they approach him with their woes, and find that he runs away without looking back at them, they are filled with indignation and talk of the discrepancy between word and deed. Whereas the fact is, the singer has more than enough woes of his own, and he sings them because he can't get rid of them. *L'uccello canta nella gabbia, non di gioia ma di rabbia,* says the Italian proverb: "The bird sings in the cage, not from joy but from rage." It is impossible to love sufferers, particularly hopeless sufferers, and whoever says otherwise is a deliberate liar. "Come unto Me all ye that labour and are heavy laden, and I will give you rest." But you remember what the Jews said about Him: "He speaks as one having authority!" And if Jesus had been unable, or *had not possessed the right*, to answer this sceptical taunt, He would have had to renounce His words. We common mortals have neither divine powers nor divine rights, we can only love our neighbours whilst they still have hope, and any pretence of going beyond this is empty swagger. Ask him who sings of suffering for nothing but his songs. Rather think of alleviating his burden than of requiring alleviation from him. Surely not for ever should we ask any poet to sob and look upon tears. I will end with another Italian saying: *Non è un si triste cane che non meni la coda.* . . . "No dog so wretched but he wags his tail sometimes."

43

If a patient fulfils all the orders of a sensible doctor, we say he behaves wisely. If he wantonly neglects his treatment, we say he acts stupidly. If a healthy person wished to inoculate himself with some dangerous disease—say phthisis—we should say he was mad, and forcibly restrain him. To such an extent are we convinced

224

that disease is evil, health good. Well—
on what is our conviction based? At a
glance the question seems absurd. But
then at a glance people would absolutely
refuse to doubt the fixity of the earth, at a
glance an ordinary person would giggle
if he was shown the problem of the relation
between the real world and the ideal.
Who knows what would seem amenable
to discussion to the ordinary person? The
philosopher has no right to appeal to the
ordinary person. The philosopher must
doubt and doubt and doubt, and question
when nobody questions, and risk making
a laughing-stock of himself. If common
sense were enough to settle all problems,
we should have known everything long
age. So that—why do we value health
more than sickness? Or even further—
which is better, health or sickness. If
we will drop the utilitarian point of view—
and all are agreed that this has no place
in philosophy—then we shall see at once
that we have no grounds whatever for
preferring health and sickness. We have
invented neither the one nor the other. We
found them both in the world along with
us. Why then do we, who know so little
about it, take upon ourselves to judge

which are nature's successes, which her failures ? Health is agreeable—sickness disagreeable. But this consideration is unworthy of a philosopher : otherwise why be a philosopher, why distinguish oneself from the herd ? The philosopher invented morality, which has at its disposal various pure ideas that have no relation to empirical life. Then let us go further. Reason should have a supply of pure ideas also. Let Reason judge in her own independent way, without conforming to conventional ideas. When she has no other resort, let her proceed by the method of negation : everything that common sense asserts, I, Reason, declare to be false. So—common sense says sickness is bad, reason therefore asserts that sickness is the highest boon. Such Reason we should call autonomous, law-unto-itself. Like a real monarch, it is guided only by its own will. Let all considerations point in favour of health, Reason must remain inexorable and keep her stand till we are all brought to obedience. She must praise suffering, deformity, failure, hopelessness. At every step she must fight commonsense and utilitarianism, until mankind is brought under. Is she afraid of rebellion ? Must she in the last issue, like

226

morality, adapt herself to the inclinations
of the mob ?

44

Experience and Science.—As we are well
aware, science does not, nay cannot, admit
experience in all its extent. She throws
overboard an enormous quantity of
individual facts, regarding them as the
ballast of our human vessel. She takes note
only of such phenomena as alternate constantly and with a certain regularity. Best
of all she likes those phenomena which can
be artificially provoked, when, so to speak,
experiment is possible. She explains the
rotation of the earth and succession of
the seasons since a regular recurrence is
observable, and she demonstrates thunder
and lightning with a spark from an electric
machine. In a word, in so far as a regular
alternation of phenomena is observable,
so far extends the realm of science. But
what about those individual phenomena
which do not recur, and which cannot be
artificially provoked ? If all men were
blind, and one for a moment recovered
his sight and opened his eyes on God's
world, science would reject his evidence.
Yet the evidence of one seeing man is worth
that of a million blind. Sudden enlighten-

ments are possible in our life—even if they endure only for a few seconds. Must they be passed over in silence because they are not normal and cannot be provoked ?— or treated poetically, as beautiful fictions ? Science insists on it. She declares that no judgments are true except such as can be verified by all and everyone. She exceeds her bounds. Experience is wider than scientific experiment, and individual phenomena mean much more to us than the constantly recurrent.

Science is useful—but she need not pretend to truth. She cannot know what truth is, she can only accumulate universal laws. Whereas there are, and always have been, non-scientific ways of searching for truth, ways which lead, if not to the innermost secrets, yet to the threshold. These roads, however, we have let fall into ruin whilst we followed our modern methodologies, so now we dare not even think of them. What gives us the right to assert that astrologers, alchemists, diviners, and sorcerers who passed the long nights alone with their thoughts, wasted their time in vain ? As for the philosopher's stone, that was merely a plausible excuse invented to satisfy the uninitiated. Could an alchemist dare to confess openly that all his efforts were towards no useful or utilitarian end ? He had to guard against importunate curiosity and impertinent authority in outsiders. So he lied, now frightening, now alluring the mob through its cupidity. But certainly he had his own important work to do: and it had only one fault, that it was purely personal to him. And about personal matters it is considered correct to keep silent. . . . Astonishing fact ! As a rule a man hesitates over trifles. But it does sometimes occur that a moment arrives when he is filled with unheard-of courage and resolution in his judgments. He is ready to stand up for his opinions against all the world, dead or living. Whence such sudden surety, what does it mean ? Rationally we can discover no foundation for it. If a lover has got into his head that his beloved is the fairest woman on earth, worth the whole of life to him ; if one who has been insulted feels that his offender is the basest wretch, deserving torture and death ; if a would-be Columbus persuades himself that America is the only goal for his ambition—who will convince such men that their opinions, shared by none but themselves, are false or unjustifiable ? And for whose sake will they renounce their tenets ? For the sake of objective truth ? that is, for the pleasure of the assurance that all men after them will repeat their judgment for truth ? They don't care. Let Don Quixote run broadcast with drawn sword, proving the beauty of Dulcinea or the impending horror of windmills. As a matter of fact, he and the German philosophers with him have a vague idea, a kind of presentiment, that their giants are but mill-sails, and that their ideal on the whole is but a common girl driving swine to pasture. To defy such deadly doubt they take to the sword or to argument, and do not rest until they have succeeded in stopping the mouth of everybody. When from all lips they hear the praise of Dulcinea they say : yes, she is beautiful, and she never drove pigs. When the world beholds their windmilling exploits with amazement they are filled with triumph ; sheep are not sheep, mills are not mills, as you might imagine ; they are knights and cyclops. This is called a proven, all-binding, universal truth. The support of the mob is a necessary condition of the existence of modern philosophy and its knights of the woful countenance. Scientific philosophy wearies

for a new Cervantes who will put a stop to
its paving the way to truth by dint of
argument. All opinions have a right to
exist, and if we speak of privilege, then
preference should be given to such as are
most run down to-day ; namely, to such
opinions as cannot be verified and which
are, for that selfsame reason, universal.
Once, long ago " man invented speech in
order to express his real relation to the
universe." So he may be heard, even though
the relation he wishes to express be unique,
not to verified by any other individual.
To attempt to verify it by observations
and experiments is strictly forbidden. If
the habit of " objective verification " has
destroyed your native receptivity to such
an extent that your eyes and ears are gone,
and you must rely only on the evidence of
instruments or objects not subject to your
will, then, of course, nothing is left you
but to stick to the belief that science is
perfect knowledge. But if your eyes live
and your ear is sensitive—throw away
instruments and apparatuses, forget
methodology and scientific Don-Quixotism,
and try to trust yourself. What harm
is there in not having universal judgments
or truths ? How will it hurt you to see

sheep as sheep ? It is a step forward. You will learn not to see with everybody's eyes, but to see as none other sees. You will learn not to meditate, but to conjure up and call forth with words alien to all but yourself an unknown beauty and an unheard-of power. Not for nothing, I repeat, did astrologers and alchemists scorn the experimental method—which, by the way, far from being anything new or particularly modern, is as old as the hills. Animals experiment, though they do not compose treatises on inductive logic or pride themselves on their reasoning powers. A cow who has burnt her mouth in her trough will come up cautiously next time to feed. Every experimenter is the same— only he systematises. But animals can often trust to instinct when experience is lacking. And have we humans got sufficient experience ? Can experience give us what we want most ? If so, let science and craftsmanship serve our everyday need, let even philosophy, also eager to serve, go on finding universal truths. But beyond craft, science, and philosophy there is another region of knowledge. Through all the ages men, each one at his own risk, have sought to penetrate into this region. Shall we,

men of the twentieth century, voluntarily
renounce our supreme powers and rights,
and because public opinion demands it,
occupy ourselves exclusively with discovering useful information ? Or, in order not
to appear mean or poverty-stricken in our
own eyes, shall we accept in place of the
philosopher's stone our modern metaphysics,
which muffles her dread of actuality in
postulates, absolutes, and such-like apparently transcendental paraphernalia ?

45

The Russian Spirit.—It will easily be
admitted that the distinguishing qualities
of Russian literature, and of Russian art
in general, are simplicity, truthfulness, and
complete lack of rhetorical ornament.
Whether it be to our credit or to our discredit
is not for me to judge, but one thing seems
certain : that our simplicity and truthfulness are due to our relatively scanty culture.
Whilst European thinkers have for centuries
been beating their brains over insoluble
problems, we have only just begun to try
our powers. We have no failures behind
us. The fathers of the profoundest Russian
writers were either landowners, dividing

their time between extravagant amusement
and State service, or peasants whose drudgery
left them no time for idle curiosity. Such
being the case, how can we know whether
human knowledge has any limits ? And if
we don't know, it seems to us it is only
because we haven't tried to find out. Other
people's experience is not ours. We are
not bound by their conclusions. Indeed,
what do we know of the experience of others,
save what we gather, very vaguely and
fragmentarily and unreliably, from books ?
It is natural for us to believe the best,
till the contrary is proved to us. Any
attempt to deprive us of our belief meets
with the most energetic resistance.

The most sceptical Russian hides a hope
at the bottom of his soul. Hence our
fearlessness of the truth, realistic truth which
so stunned European critics. Realism was
invented in the West, established there as
a theory. But in the West, to counteract
it, were invented numberless other palli-
ating theories whose business it was to
soften down the disconsolate conclusions of
Realism. There in Europe they have the
être suprême, the *deus sive natura*, Hegel's
absolute, Kant's postulates, English utilitarianism, progress, humanitarianism,

hundreds of philosophic and sociological theories in which even extreme realists can so cleverly dish up what they call life, that life, or realism, ceases to be life or reality altogether.

The Westerner is self-reliant. He knows that if he doesn't help himself nobody will help him. So he directs all his thoughts to making the best of his opportunities. A limited time is granted him. If he can't get to the end of his song within the time-limit, the song must remain unsung. Fate will not give him one minute's grace for the unbeaten bars. Therefore as an experienced musician he adapts himself superbly. Not a second is wasted. The *tempo* must not drag for an instant, or he is lost. The *tempo* is everything, and it exacts facility and quickness of movement. During a few short beats the artist must produce many notes, and produce them so as to leave the impression that he was not hurried, that he had all the time in the world at his disposal. Moreover, each note must be complete, accomplished, have its fulness and its value. Native talent alone will not suffice for this. Experience is necessary, tradition, training, and inherited instinct. *Carpe diem*—the European has been living up to the motto for two thousand years. But if we Russians are convinced of anything, it is that we have time enough and to spare. To count days, much less hours and minutes—find me the Russian who could demean himself to such a bourgeois occupation. We look round, we stretch ourselves, we rub our eyes, we want first of all to decide what we shall do, and how we shall do it, before we can begin to live in earnest. We don't choose to decide anyhow, nor at second-hand, from fragments of other people's information. It must be from our own experience, with our own brains, that we judge. We admit no traditions. In no literature has there been such a determined struggle with tradition as in ours. We have wanted to re-examine everything, re-state everything. I won't deny that our courage is drawn from our quite uncultured confidence in our own powers. Byelinsky, a half-baked undergraduate, deriving his knowledge of European philosophy at third hand, began a quarrel with the universe over the long-forgotten victims of Philip II. and the Inquisition. In that quarrel is the sense and essence of all creative Russian literature. Dostoevsky, towards his end, raised the same storm and the same question over the little tear of an unfortunate child.

A Russian believes he can do anything, hence he is afraid of nothing. He paints life in the gloomiest colours—and were you to ask him : How can you accept such a life ? how can you reconcile yourself with such horrors of reality as have been described by all your writers, from Poushkin to Tchekhov ? he would answer in the words of Dmitri Karamazov: *I do not accept life.* This answer seems at first sight absurd. Since life is here, impossible not to accept it. But there is a sub-meaning in the reply, a lingering belief in the possibility of a final triumph over " evil." In the strength of this belief the Russian goes forth to meet his enemy—he does not hide from him. Our sectarians immolate themselves. Tolstoyans and votaries of the various sects that crop up so plentifully in Russia go in among the people, they go, God knows to what lengths, destroying their own lives and the lives of others. Writers do not lag behind sectarians. They, too, refuse to be prudent, to count the cost or the hours. Minutes, seconds, time-beats, all this is so insignificant as to be invisible to the naked eye. We wish to draw with a generous

237

hand from fathomless eternity, and all that is limited we leave to European bourgeoisie. With few exceptions Russian writers really despise the pettiness of the West. Even those who have admired Europe most have done so because they failed most completely to understand her. They did not want to understand her. That is why we have always taken over European ideas in such fantastic forms. Take the sixties for example. With its loud ideas of sobriety and modest outlook, it was a most drunken period. Those who awaited the New Messiah and the Second Advent read Darwin and dissected frogs. It is the same to-day. We allow ourselves the greatest luxury that man can dream of—sincerity, truthfulness —as if we were spiritual Crœsuses, as if we had plenty of everything, could afford to let everything be seen, ashamed of nothing. But even Crœsuses, the greatest sovereigns of the world, did not consider they had the right to tell the truth at all times. Even kings have to pretend—think of diplomacy. Whereas, we think we may speak the truth, and the truth only, that any lie which obscures our true substance is a crime; since our true substance is the world's finest treasure, its finest reality. . . .

Tell this to a European, and it will seem a joke to him, even if he can grasp it at all. A European uses all his powers of intellect and talent, all his knowledge and his art for the purpose of concealing his real self and all that really affects him :—for that the natural is ugly and repulsive, no one in Europe will dispute for a moment. Not only the fine arts, but science and philosophy in Europe tell lies instinctively, by lying they justify their existence. First and last, a European student presents you with a finished theory. Well, and what does all the " finish " and the completeness signify ? It merely means that none of our western neighbours will end his speech before the last reassuring word is said ; he will never let nature have the last word ; so he rounds off his synthesis. With him, ornament and rhetoric is a *sine qua non* of creative utterance, the only remedy against all ills. In philosophy reigns theodicy, in science, the law of sequence. Even Kant could not avoid declamation, even with him the last word is " moral necessity." Thus there lies before us the choice between the artistic and accomplished lie of old, cultured Europe, a lie which is the outcome of a thousand years of hard and bitter effort, and the

239

artless, sincere simplicity of young, uncultured Russia.

They are nearer the end, we are nearer the beginning. And which is nearer the truth ? And can there be a question of voluntary, free choice ? Probably neither the old age of Europe nor the youth of Russia can give us the truth we seek. But does such a thing as ultimate truth exist ? Is not the very conception of truth, the very assumption of the possibility of truth, merely an outcome of our limited experience, a fruit of limitation ? We decide *a priori* that one thing must be possible, another impossible, and from our arbitrary assumptions we proceed to deduce the body of truth. Each one judges in his own way, according to his powers and the conditions of his existence. The timid, scared man worries after *order*, that will give him a day of peace and quiet, youth dreams of beauty and brilliance, old age doesn't want to think of anything, having lost the faculty for hope. And so it goes on, *ad infinitum*. And this is called truth, truths ! Every man thinks that his own experience covers the whole range of life. And, therefore, the only men who turn out to be at all in the right are empiricists and positivists. There can be no question of truth once we tear ourselves away from the actual conditions of life.

Our confident truthfulness, like European rhetoric, turns out to be " beyond truth and falsehood." The young East and the old West alike suffer from the restrictions imposed by truth—but the former ignores the restrictions, whilst the latter adapts itself to them. After all, it comes to pretty much the same in the end. Is not clever rhetoric as delightful as truthfulness ? Each is equally *life*. Only we find unendurable a rhetoric which poses as truth, and a truthfulness which would appear cultured. Such a masquerade would try to make us believe that truth, which is only *limitedness*, has a real objective existence. Which is offensive. Until the contrary is proved, we need to think that only one assertion has or can have any objective reality : *that nothing on earth is impossible.* Every time somebody wants to force us to admit that there are other, more limited and limiting truths, we must resist with every means we can lay hands on. We do not hesitate even to make use of morality and logic, both of which we have abused so often. But why not use them !

When a man is at his last resources,

he does not care what weapons he picks up.

46

Nur für Schwindelfreie.—To be proper, I ought to finish with a moral. I ought to say to the reader that in spite of all I have said, or perhaps *because of* all I have said—for in conclusions, as you are aware, "in spite of" is always interchangeable with "because of," particularly if the conclusion be drawn from many scattered data —well then, because of all I have said, hope is not lost. Every destruction leads to construction, sweet rest follows labour, dawn follows the darkest hour, and so on and so on and so on—all the banalities with which a writer reconciles his reader. But it is never too late for reconciliation, and it is often too early. So why not postpone the moral for a few years—even a few dozen years, God granting us the length of life? Why make the inevitable "conclusion" at the end of every book? I am almost certain that sooner or later I can promise the reader all his heart desires. But not yet. He may, of course, dispense with my consolations. What do promises matter, anyhow? especially when neither reader nor writer can fulfil them. But if there is no escape, if a writer is finally obliged to admit in everybody's hearing that the secret desires of poor mankind may yet be realised, let 'us at least give the wretched writer a respite, let him postpone his confession till old age—*usque ad infinitum*. . . . Meanwhile our motto " *Nur für Schwindelfreie*." There are in the Alps narrow, precipitous paths where only mountaineers may go, who feel no giddiness. Giddy-free! " Only for the giddy-free," it says on the noticeboard. He who is subject to giddiness takes a broad, safe road, or sits away below and admires the snowy summits. Is it inevitably necessary to mount up ? Beyond the snow-line are no fat pastures nor goldfields. They say that up there is to be found the clue to the eternal mystery—but they say so many things. We can't believe everything. He who is tired of the valleys, loves climbing, and is not afraid to look down a precipice, and, most of all, has nothing left in life but the " metaphysical craving," he will certainly climb to the summits without asking what awaits him there. He does not fear, he longs for giddiness. But he will hardly call people after him : he doesn't want just anybody for a companion. In such a case companions are not wanted at all, much less those tender-footed ones who are used to every convenience, roads, street lamps, guide-posts, careful maps which mark every change in the road ahead. They will not help, only hinder. They will prove superfluous, heavy ballast, which may not be thrown overboard. Fuss over them, console them, promise them! Who would be bothered? Is it not better to go one's way alone, and not only to refrain from enticing others to follow, but frighten them off as much as possible, exaggerate every danger and difficulty? In order that conscience may not prick too hard—we who love high altitudes love a quiet conscience—let us find a justification for their inactivity. Let us tell them they are the best, the worthiest of people, really the salt of the earth. Let us pay them every possible mark of respect. But since they are subject to giddiness, they had better stay down. The upper Alpine ways, as any guide will tell you, are *nur für Schwindelfreie*.

THE LONDON AND NORWICH PRESS, LIMITED, LONDON AND NORWICH, ENGLAND

CPSIA information can be obtained
at www.ICGtesting.com
Printed in the USA
BVHW060200280820
587365BV00002B/155